# CHESHIRE FOLK SONGS
## & ASSOCIATED TRADITIONS

# CHESHIRE FOLK SONGS

## & ASSOCIATED TRADITIONS

**Compiled and edited by**

**ROY CLINGING**

Léonie Press

ISBN: 1 901253 49 X ISBN13: 978-1-901253-49-8

Published May 2005
Reprinted March 2006
Reprinted May 2008
Reprinted March 2011



British Library Cataloguing in Publication Data.
A catalogue record for this book is available from the British Library.

Published by
Léonie Press
13 Vale Road, Hartford,
Northwich, Cheshire CW8 1PL
Great Britain
Tel: +44 (0) 1606 75660
email: anne@leoniepress.com
Website: www.leoniepress.com

Printed by
Poplar Services, St Helens
Covers laminated by The Finishing Touch, St Helens

*Roy Clinging*

# About the Author

Roy Clinging has been seriously involved in folk music since the early 1970s and is now a full time performer with experience of clubs and festivals across the UK and in the USA. He has been instrumental in setting up and organising a number of folk clubs and other events in the Chester area and still maintains strong contacts with his local gang of Soulers, with whom he once regularly performed, and is an active member of the Chester City Morris Men. Having always had a specific interest in his local culture he is a member of the English Folk Dance & Song Society and although this is his first book he has a number of CD recordings to his credit – *Cheshire Born* (1999), an anthology of Cheshire songs and tunes, *An Honest Working Man* (2001), a more general collection of folk songs and tunes from around the country, *Another Round* (2005) with fiddler Neil Brookes, and *When This Old Hat was New* (2010), a collection of 19th century songs and tunes with The Hat Show Band.

# CONTENTS

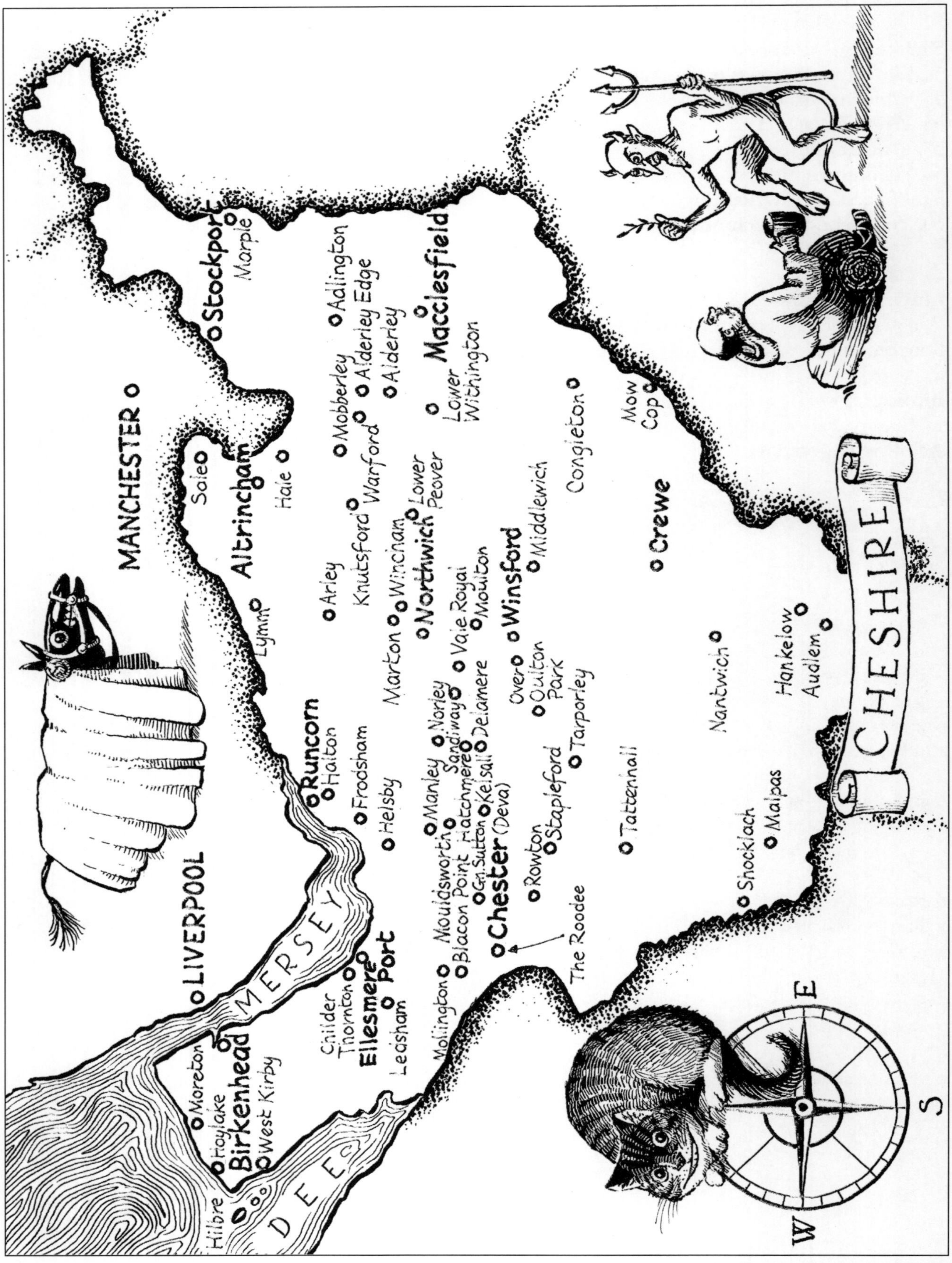
CHESHIRE
MANCHESTER
LIVERPOOL
MERSEY
DEE
Hilbre
Hoylake
Moreton
Birkenhead
West Kirby
Childer Thornton
Ellesmere Port
Ledsham
Mollington
Blacon Point
Chester (Deva)
The Roodee
Mouldsworth
Manley
Hatchmere
Gt. Sutton
Kelsall
Delamere
Sandiway
Norley
Rowton
Stapleford
Tarporley
Tattenhall
Shocklach
Malpas
Runcorn
Halton
Frodsham
Helsby
Marton
Over
Oulton Park
Vale Royal
Moulton
Winsford
Nantwich
Hankelow
Audlem
Lymm
Arley
Knutsford
Wincham
Northwich
Middlewich
Crewe
Altrincham
Sale
Hale
Warford
Lower Peover
Congleton
Mobberley
Alderley Edge
Alderley
Lower Withington
Mow Cop
Stockport
Marple
Adlington
Macclesfield
W
S
E

# INTRODUCTION

Whenever I was ill as a child my grandmother would sit by my bed and sing to me and although to my eternal discredit I can remember nothing of any real consequence, it gave me an early contact with folk song, and an interest that I still hold to this day. One of her favourite rhymes was the slightly dubious:

*Old Mon o' Mow,*[1]
*Sitting on his po,*
*Eating apple dumplings*
*Yo yo yo*

The only other snippet I can recall from those formative years is:

*Mary Ellen at the church turned up.*
*Her ma turned up, and her pa turned up.*
*Her sister Gert, her rich uncle Bert,*
*And the parson with his long white shirt turned up.*
*No bridegroom at the church turnèd up,*
*But the telegram boy with his nose turned up*
*With a telegram to say that they couldn't wed today,*
*'Cos they found him in the river with his toes turned up!*

I used to feel quite guilty that I was unable to remember any more of my grandmother's songs, but a recent conversation with my mother put my mind more at ease. It seems that although my grandmother sang a great deal, often while going about her daily tasks, she never actually knew any complete songs – only snatches. It was her mother, my great-grandmother, who had the folk song repertoire and it seems that she would regularly entertain family and friends with her songs, accompanying herself on the concertina. It was, therefore, my grandmother and not me who failed to recall these songs properly as I was still a baby when my great-grandmother died. What a relief!

As I grew up my interest in folk music deepened firstly by listening to recordings of some of the pioneers of what we now call 'the folk revival', and then progressing to becoming more actively involved through folk clubs, festivals, country dances, morris dancing and souling. I first experienced the tradition of souling, and with it my first Cheshire folk song, shortly after I moved from Middlewich to Chester in the early 1970s. Souling, or soul-caking, is the Cheshire form of a mumming play and was, at one time, widespread throughout the county. Singing is frequently an integral part of souling and, true to form, we began each performance with two verses of a song outside the venue before the *Enterer In* burst into the room to announce the impending appearance of the actors. At the end of the play we would sing more verses as we went around the room collecting money (in our case for local charities) and left while still singing *'And we'll come no more a-souling until another year.'*

After listening to, and learning from, singers from most other parts of the UK, it was something of a defining moment for me when I realised that if souling songs still existed, there might be others. What if there were more songs and traditions from my own little corner of the country that were just as varied and interesting as those I'd heard about from other people, or read about in books? My curiosity had to be satisfied. I decided that all the material should have at least some connection with Cheshire – although in some cases this may be rather tenuous – and be either from or about

[1] The *Old Mon o' Mow* is a 65 foot high stone pillar on a hill called Mow Cop on the Cheshire / Staffordshire border. On the site of an ancient cairn it was created by centuries of quarrying the stone all around it, though why this single pillar was left standing is unclear.

people and places within the old county boundaries. I realise that some locations now come under the more generic headings of *'Merseyside'* or *'Greater Manchester'*, but while this material was still in common usage it was, and still is to many of us, Cheshire.

I was pleased then to find that in 1826 Roger Wilbraham, a local historian, had written in his modestly titled work *An Attempt at a Glossary of Some Words Used in Cheshire*:

> *'The County Palatine of Chester having been in great measure a separate jurisdiction till the days of Queen Elizabeth, had very little intercourse with the neighbouring counties; the principal families of the county, and much more those in a middle station in life, for the most past intermarried among each other – a practice which is recommended in an old Cheshire adage[2]; so that the original customs and manners, as well as the old language of the county have received less changes and innovations than those in most other parts of England.'*

This may have been so in 1826, but it is far less apparent as we enter the 21st century. In the nineteenth, and even early twentieth century, folk songs and customs, especially in largely rural communities, were still widespread and many people sang almost as part of their way of life. The 1914 - 1918 conflict changed it all, however, as apart from the fact that many of the people who knew the old ways were killed, those that were left just hadn't the heart to revive old memories. It is to our benefit then, that a few scholars took it upon themselves to note down and record this music for posterity, although their task was not such an easy one as it may sound. The songs themselves were in greater abundance than they are nowadays, but the singers were not always so willing to part with them and class barriers kept the working man's music out of reach of polite society. One of the most prolific collectors of the period, Cecil Sharp (1859 - 1924), noted his first song in Hambridge, Somerset, in 1903 when, by pure chance, he heard gardener John England singing *The Seeds of Love*. A L Lloyd (*Folk Song in England*, 1967) takes up the story:

> *'So Sharp's friend Charles Marson, a Christian socialist vicar with unusually keen sympathy for his flock, was forced to declare: "The folk-song is like the duck-billed platypus in this particular, you can live for years within a few yards of it and never suspect its existence." He confessed that eight years of constant residence in the small village of Hambridge, in Somerset, had left him "in Stygian ignorance of the wealth of Art which that village contained. Only one song, and that by chance, had fallen upon his untouched ears." Yet hundreds of songs turned up there and in surrounding villages once Sharp got to work. Surprising? Not at all. Till recently, working people have generally hidden their most precious cultural possessions from the master, the squire, the parson. "Intimacy with a peasant may go a long way and yet stop short of his songs", says Sharp. So contact between collector and singer tended to be rather less than candid because, however civil, each approached the other gingerly across a social chasm.'*

It was never going to be easy then, especially as Cheshire does not have an obvious folk culture as is the case with, say, Lancashire, Yorkshire, or the North East of England, nor was it seen as a haven for song collecting when such activities were at their peak. It is also interesting to note that while many of the major figures in the field are represented in this volume – The Rev Sabine Baring-Gould (1834 - 1924), Frank Kidson (1855 - 1926), Lucy Broadwood (1858 - 1929), and the aforementioned Cecil Sharp – their impact is minimal.

In *The Cheshire Round* (Vol 1 No 5, 1966, pp 134-137), an article by Geoffrey Nulty makes reference to a number of songs and tunes which are no longer in current usage, and mourns their passing. Some of these I have encountered on my travels and are therefore included in this collection (*The Cheshire Cheese, The Spanish Lady's Love*); others however, have constantly eluded me. Nulty mentions a dance tune known as *The Cheshire Archers* which:

---

[2] The adage in question is *'better wed over the mixen than over the moor'* A 'mixen' is a midden and the saying implies that it is safer to marry someone local than mix with a stranger.

*'Is said to have been popular until the battle of Blore Heath* [1459] *in the Wars of the Roses, when the Cheshire archers wearing the emblem of a white swan fought for Queen Margaret. Their deathroll was so great that Cheshire was in mourning for generations, never again singing and dancing to the tune which celebrated the feats of the archers.'*

This is just one of a number of songs or tunes that I have seen or heard references to, but have not yet been able to uncover in any reasonable form.

It would appear though that I am not the only one who has had trouble unearthing some of the county's cultural gems. In 1866, Egerton Leigh, when writing the preface to *Ballads and Legends of Cheshire*, expressed disappointment at the lack of material he had to draw on, suggesting the invention of printing as a major influence.

*'Printing put an end to the story-teller's occupation; but at the time the live books were discarded, the new art did not, whilst there was yet time, collect the stories of oral tradition, and the treasures of auld lang syne, and preserve and pot them for posterity.'*

Much of the material in Egerton Leigh's book was contributed by other noted figures of the time, though it is not always clear whether these people were submitting material for publication or writing it themselves. In many cases I suspect the latter as the style of some of the verse is very much of the period. This, however, has not prevented me from raiding the contents of this volume as, apart from some useful items reprinted from earlier works, it is an excellent source of local stories, legends and superstitions.

Despite the gloomy picture this may paint, the whole project has been a hugely enjoyable one, and I have had the pleasure of meeting and exchanging ideas and information with some wonderful people along the way. While my main interest has always been folk song, and that remains the main focus of the book, I have felt it prudent to include a little information on some of the great variety of traditions and customs at one time prevalent in the area. The main reason for this is that in many cases, such as souling, pace egging and May singing, the songs and their associated practices are almost inextricably linked. Others, however, are just snippets of information that I have come across in my research and thought to be of interest. While I hope that there is sufficient material here to interest if not the folk academic, then at least the folk enthusiast, and that some new and unfamiliar ground is being covered, it is by no means intended to be exclusive. These are the songs and customs of the people and, as such, they belong to us all.

Of the 60 songs given, 10 are printed as text only, 8 have been found as words only and a tune added later, 12 are relatively recent compositions, and the remaining 31 have been found with words and tune together in a singable form. The songs have been researched in libraries and archives, sent to me by interested individuals or recorded from local singers. I have made every effort to cite my sources of information with as much background as is known, while trying to keep the style and notes fairly informal.

The folk songs of any area are dependent on the people who sing them and keep them alive and without these often isolated groups or individuals we would have no folk/traditional music at all. These people have my undying admiration.

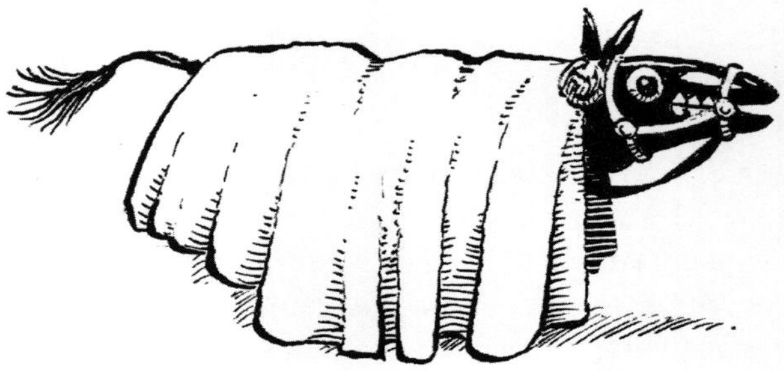

# 1. The Alderley Lasses

Here's a health to the Alderley Lasses
The dark and the fair and the brown
Come lads fill up quickly your glasses
Here's to each you love best in the town

Not forgetting the lasses of Warford
The growing as well as the grown
May they find wheresoever it's offered
A hand and a heart like their own

Here's to all whatsoever we call them
Our Sarahs and Betsies and Janes
May the evils of life ne'er befall them
Its sorrows, its perils or pains

But tho' famed as we think for their beauty
May their personal charms be surpassed
By their graces of virtue and duty
Attractions more certain to last

Then kind heaven will give them its blessing
May they prosper in all that they do
And then every sweetheart addressing
Will surely prove constant and true

Then moreo'er I am sure that the Rector
Will marry them all when he can
If so be, that they take for protector
An honest good Alderley man.

In 1803, after 25 years of service, the Rector of Alderley, the Rev Edward Stanley, invited every householder in Alderley to a feast. This was, apparently, one of three songs composed by Mr Stanley to be sung at this festive occasion.

# 2. Alderley Mummers' Song

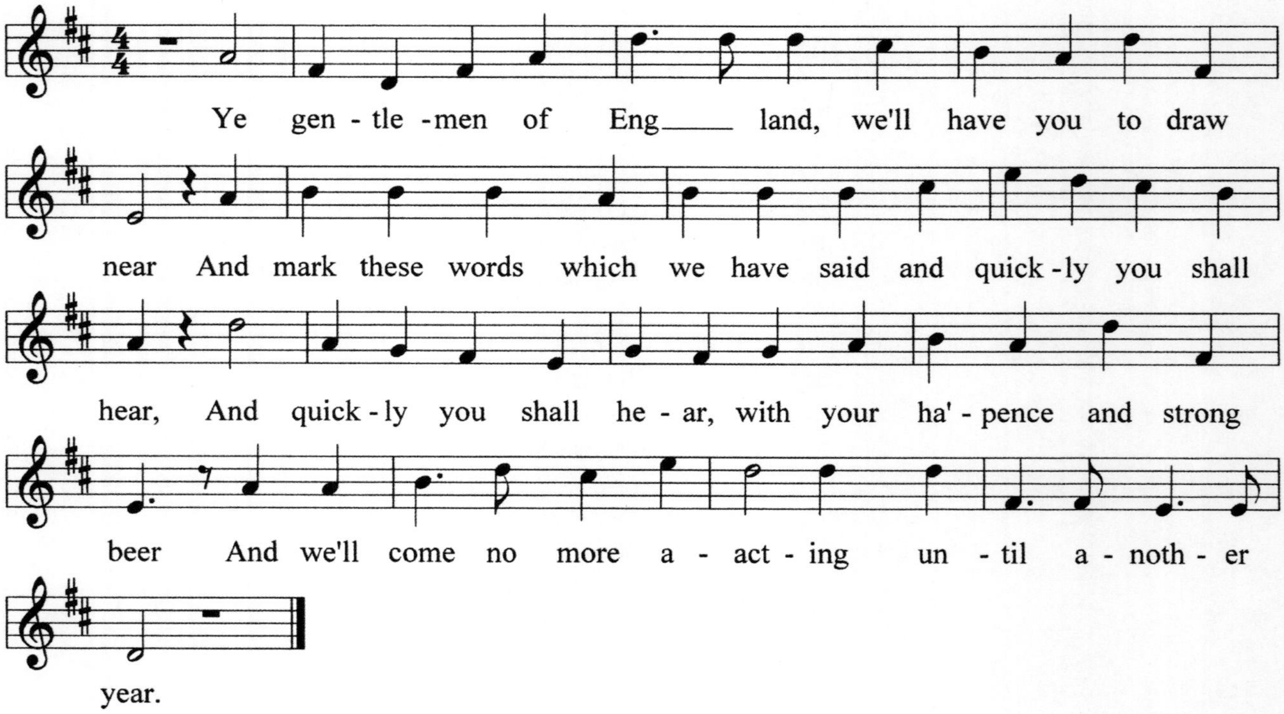


Ye gentlemen of England, we'll have you to draw near
And mark these words which we have said and quickly you shall hear;
And quickly you shall hear, with your ha'pence and strong beer
And we'll come no more a-acting until another year.

The winter it is coming on, dark, dirty, wet and cold
And for to try your good nature, this night we do make bold;
This night we do make bold, with your ha'pence and strong beer
And we'll come no more a-acting until another year.

Go down into your cellar and see what you can find.
If your barrels be not empty, we hope you will prove kind;
We hope you will prove kind with your ha'pence and strong beer
And we'll come no more a-acting until another year.

God bless the master of this house and the mist-er-ess also,
And all your little children that around your table go.
Likewise your men and maidens, your cattle and your store
And all that lies within your gates, we wish them ten times more;
We wish them ten times more, with your ha'pence and strong beer
For we'll come no more a-acting until another year.

So now we make an ending of what we have begun,
For a-going a-acting we think there is no sin;
We think there is no sin, with your ha'pence and strong beer
And we'll come no more a-acting until another year.

The Alderley Mummers' play was performed in the tenants' hall on the Alderley Park estate of Lord and Lady Stanley as part of the Christmas celebrations and members of the Barber family, who were tenants on the estate, took all the parts. Their last performance was in 1937 after which the estate was sold. There is no real difference between mumming and souling [see notes to *Souling Song*] – except, of course, the time of year – and this version, with very few changes, is still currently in use not only by the present Alderley Mummers, but also by the Jones' Ale Soulcakers of Chester. The soulers perform in the pubs in and around Chester in late October/early November, singing the first two verses outside the door before the play begins and the rest of the song as they are leaving. The Alderley men go out over Christmas and New Year sticking closer to the collected script and singing the whole song at the end of the play.

# 3. Blue Cap

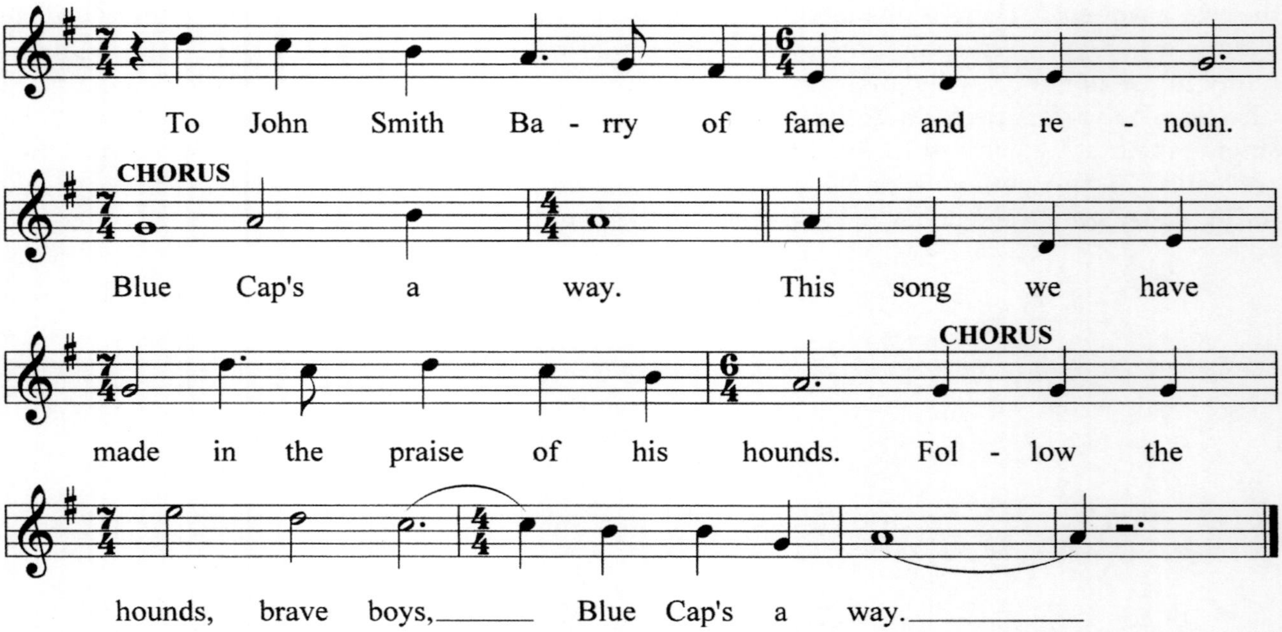


To John Smith Barry of fame and renown;  
*Blue Cap's away,*  
This song we have made in the praise of his hounds.  
*Follow the hounds, brave boys, Blue Cap's away.*

Blue Cap, their leader, we'll boast of his breed;  
*Blue Cap's away,*  
No hound match his courage, no hare match his speed.  
*Follow the hounds, brave boys, Blue Cap's away.*

Hatchmere and Delamere, Budworth and back;  
Out of sound of the horn, out of sight of the pack.

To slack his pace they have fitted a drag;  
From Whitegate to Winsford to high Beeston Crag.

He was tried against Wanton whose speed was renowned;  
At Newmarket raced for five hundred pounds.

From point to point run the course all around;  
He licked the dog Wanton right into the ground.

Let those who challenge or follow him still;  
Enquire at *The Blue Cap* on Sandiway Hill.

There lift up your tankard and pass the toast round;  
Here's a health unto Blue Cap and all Cheshire hounds.

Owned by John Smith Barry, *Blue Cap* was an exceptional Cheshire foxhound that passed into legend by winning a race against the hound *Wanton*, owned by Smith Barry's greatest rival. When *Blue Cap* died in 1772, at the age of thirteen, his owner erected a monument in his honour and, from the nineteenth century at least, the name has continued to be remembered by *The Blue Cap Hotel*, in Sandiway. Pete and Chris Coe wrote the song.

Egerton Leigh's *Ballads and Legends of Cheshire* includes the following rhyme in his honour:

| | |
|---|---|
| ***B**luecap's remains, his dust and* | ***B**one,* |
| ***L**ie midst that meadow, green and* | ***L**one;* |
| ***U**ntired in speed he won his* | ***U**rn,* |
| ***E**'en harder than most heroes* | ***E**arn.* |
| ***C**heshire will never foxhound* | ***C**all* |
| ***A**mongst her pack, that's better,* | ***A**ll* |
| ***P**erfection, write on Bluecap's* | ***P**all.* |

# 4. The Brisk Young Widow

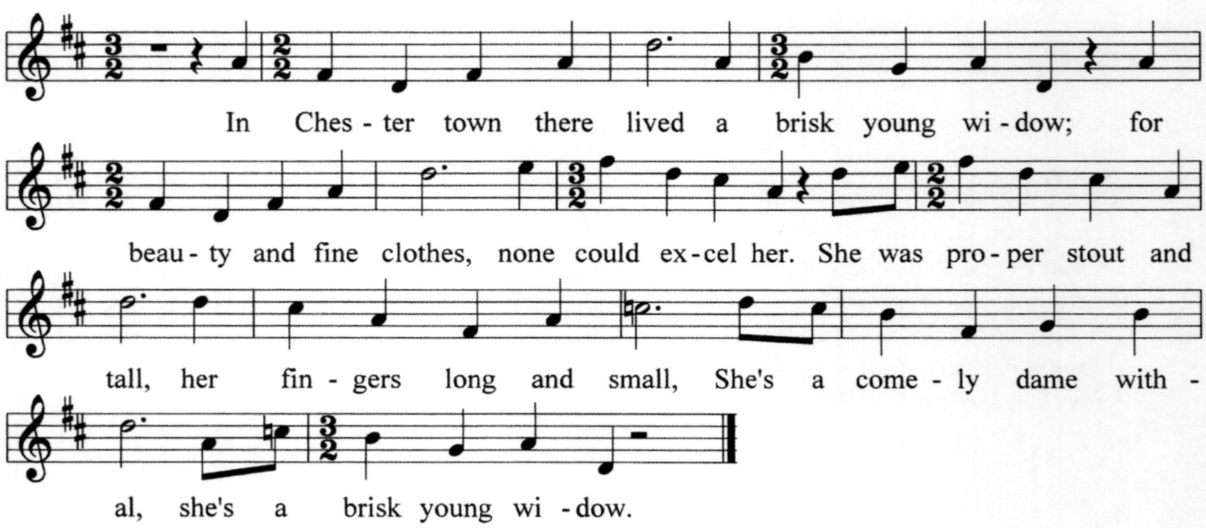


In Chester town there lived a brisk young widow;
For beauty and fine clothes, none could excel her.
She was proper stout and tall, her fingers long and small,
She's a comely dame withal, she's a brisk young widow.

A lover soon there came, a brisk young farmer,
With his hat turned up all round, thinking to gain her.
'My dear for love of you this wide world I'll go through;
If you will but prove true, you shall wed a farmer.'

Says she 'I'm not for you, nor no such fellow.
I'm for a lively lad with land and riches.
It's not your hogs and yows can maintain furbelows,
My silk and satin clothes are all my glory.'

'O madam, don't be coy for all your glory,
For fear of another day and another story.
If the world on you should frown, your topknot must come down
To a linsey-woolsey gown. Where is then your glory?'

At last there came that way a sooty collier.
With his hat bent down all round he soon did gain her.
Whereat the farmer swore 'The widow's mazed I'm sure;
And I'll never court no more a brisk young widow.'

Cecil Sharp collected this cautionary tale of the hazards that may be encountered when courting a rather haughty and unpredictable woman, from George Radford at Bridgewater Union, Somerset, in 1905. Mr Radford, who was 76 at the time, said that his father had been a great singer, but that this was the only song that he had managed to learn from him. A *topknot* was a knot or bow of ribbon worn on the top of the head by ladies towards the end of the 17th and into the 18th century. It later came to refer to a bow of ribbon worn in a lace cap. *Yows* are ewes; a *furbelow* is a flounce or pleated border of a skirt or petticoat, a showy ornament; *mazed* means complex and confusing and *linsey-woolsey* is a dress material of coarse inferior wool woven with cotton.

# 5. Cheshire Born

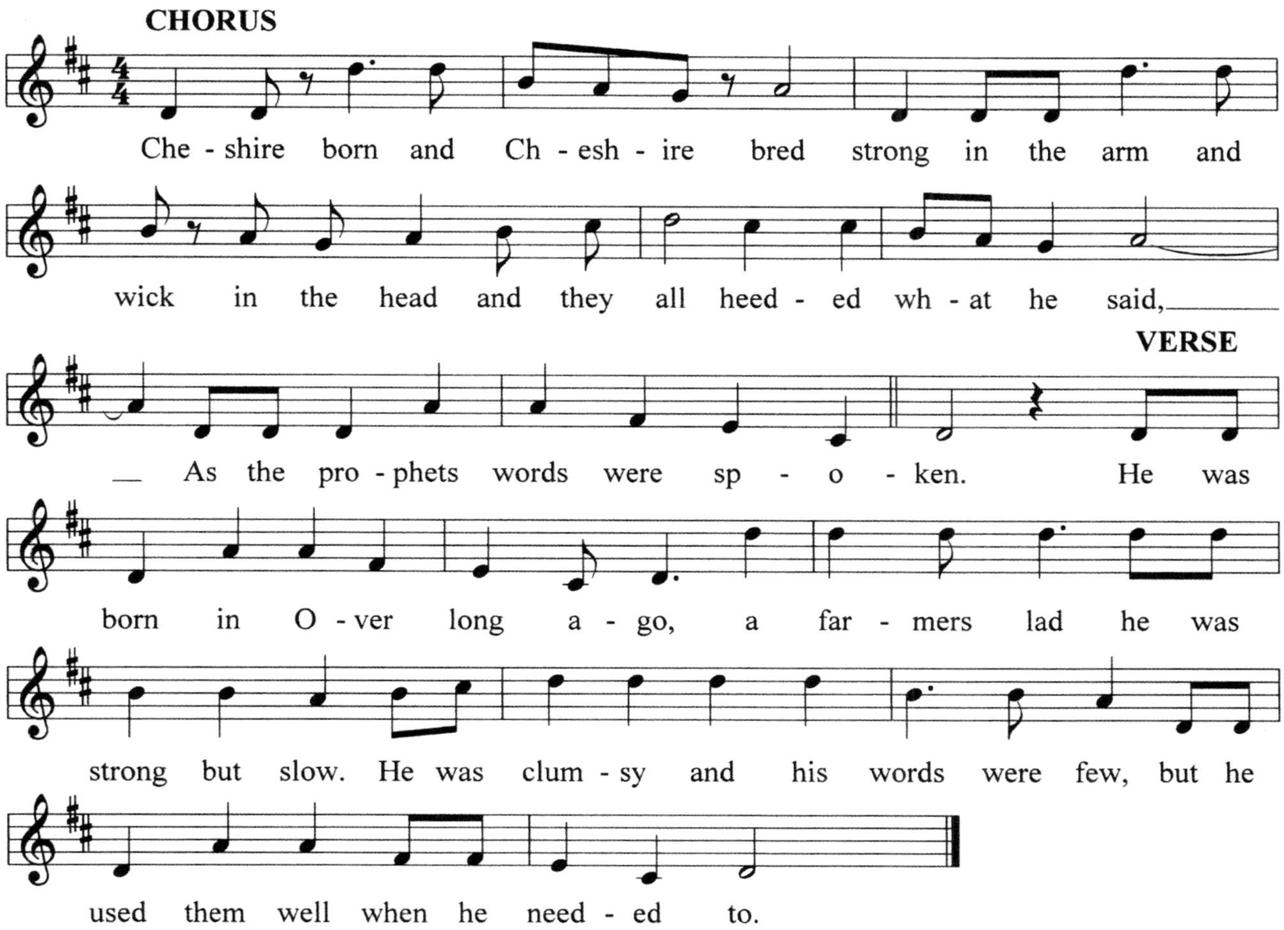


He was born in Over long ago
A farmer's lad who was strong but slow
He was clumsy and his words were few
But he used them well when he needed to.

**Chorus**: *Cheshire born and Cheshire bred*
*Strong in the arm and wick in the head*
*And they all heeded what he said*
*As the prophet's words were spoken.*

While working one fine August day,
He fell into a trance they say,
And he told of fighting fierce and proud
And how a king had lost his crown.

The news soon spread of this strange thing
And he was summoned before the king,
But the invitation scared him so,
Afraid he'd starve if he had to go.

Said the king "I like this fellow's ways,
The things he does and the things he says

So in the kitchen where it's dry and warm
He can eat and sleep and keep from harm."

But the cooks he did annoy them so
They decided he would have to go.
He was pushed in a cupboard dark and bare,
And they locked the door and left him there.

He'd kick and bang time and again,
He'd shout and scream but all in vain.
But it was here he took his final breath
And as he'd feared he starved to death.

This song refers to Robert Nixon, better known as the Cheshire Prophet. He was born in Over, near Winsford, around 1467, although the first edition of his prophecies was not published until 1714. He was a farm lad with a *'great head and goggle eyes'* and was *'extremely sulky.'* On the 22nd August 1485, he fell into a state of trance and afterwards told of visions of a great battle and how the king had been overthrown. This was the day of the battle of Bosworth Field when Henry Tudor defeated and killed Richard III, and became Henry VII. The new king heard of this and asked that Nixon be brought before him. Nixon wept at the news, saying that if he went to London he would starve. He was eventually persuaded to appear before the king who put him to the test by asking him to find a ring that he had previously hidden. Nixon replied *'He who hideth can find''*. This greatly pleased the king who, hearing of his fears, then ordered that he was to be kept in the kitchen where he would have a constant supply of food. The cooks, however, found his constant *'licking and picking at the meat'* so annoying that they locked him in a cupboard out of the way, where he was unfortunately forgotten and starved to death. *Wick* is and old word, often used in Cheshire, which means quick, or alive.

# 6. Cheshire Cavalry

Oh, come all you British heroes, and listen to my song,
To these few lines that I have penned; they won't detain you long.
Concerning of the yeomanry; their orders came that they
Should march into Liverpool on the twenty-eighth of May.

Chorus: *So let the trumpet sound as we march along the way;*
*And we marched into Liverpool on the twenty-eighth of May.*

The Cheshire Yeoman Cavalry are men of high renown,
Give credit to their country, and honour to the Crown.
Along with Colonel Egerton we'll make a gallant show,
When mounted on our warlike steeds to Liverpool we'll go.

But when the time it comes along our country for to leave,
Behold our loving sweethearts, how they lament and grieve.
We give to them a kiss and say "Farewell love, don't complain,
For I will marry you, my dear, when I return again."

Ahead Lieutenant Palin is mounted on his grey,
And when he draws his broadsword, he boldly clears the way.
There is Captain Hill, our adjutant, the truth to you I'll tell;
He boldly fought at Waterloo, where many thousands fell.

Now let a health go round, my boys, let's drink unto our Queen;
The second to our Colonel, a bumper to the brim;
The third to all our officers, in station that they be;
The fourth unto the Cheshire lads, who'll fight for liberty.

Written while at Liverpool by private John Hayward, of Stamford Bridge near Chester, this song is dated to some extent by the fact that the Earl of Chester's Yeoman Cavalry met at Liverpool for the last time in 1843, after which, on 28th May 1844, the regiment marched in for permanent duty at Chester. Colonel Egerton resigned his commission in 1847, which was followed by a meeting of his fellow officers at the George Inn, Knutsford, to prepare for his retirement, and Captain Hill retired from the adjutancy of the regiment in April 1868, after 32 years in the post. A subscription was raised among the officers past and present, with the purpose of presenting Captain Hill with *'some substantial token of the high esteem and respect in which he was held by them all, and to which his long and meritorious services appear so justly to entitle him.'* This took the form of a silver tea and coffee service, with a purse of gold.

# 7. Cheshire Cheese

A Cheshire man sailed into Spain
To trade for merchandise;
When he arrived from the main
A Spaniard him espies,
A Spaniard him espies.

Who said "You English rogue, look here
What fruits and spices fine
Our land produces twice a year
Thou hast not such in thine?
Thou hast not such in thine?"

The Cheshire man ran to his hold,
And fetched a Cheshire Cheese;
And said "Look here, you dog! behold
We have such fruits as these!
We have such fruits as these!

"Your fruits are ripe but twice a year,
As you yourself do say;
But such as I present you here
Our land brings twice a day.
Our land brings twice a day."

The Spaniard in a passion flew,
And his rapier took in hand;
The Cheshire man kicked up his heels,
Saying, "Thou art at my command!
Saying, "Thou art at my command!"

So never let a Spaniard boast,
While Cheshire men abound;
Lest they should teach him to his cost,
To dance a Cheshire Round.
To dance a Cheshire Round.

This tale of one-upmanship [see also *The Cheshire Man*] has clearly been around for a while. In *The Cheshire Sheaf* (Vol 2, August 1880, p 137), R.M. of Ledsham states that while it was originally reported that this song was published in 1746 (*Cheshire Notes and Queries* of 1897 agrees with this date), the first four verses were printed in the *Gentleman's Magazine* for March 1735.

The intricacies of dancing the *Cheshire Round*, as mentioned at the end of this song, however, remain something of a mystery, as, although descriptions of the dance exist, reports are often conflicting. In 1815 the Rector of Llanarmon wrote in *Cambrian Popular Antiquities* that he believed that the *Cheshire Round* could be traced back to the time of the Druids. He says that it is danced by two people, one of each sex, who lead off into the middle of an imaginary circle. They dance for a short time opposite each other and then with swift, lively steps chase each other around the circle. This, he asserts, has so strong a reference to the movements of the sun and moon as to leave him in no doubt that it was originally a sacred dance in their honour. Dr Rimbault, however, in *Cheshire Notes and Queries*, (vol 1, 1850 p456) says:

> *'this is a dance peculiar to the county from whence it takes its name. The musical notes of 'The Cheshire Round' may be seen in 'The Dancing Master', 1721, and in Edward Jones' 'Cheshire Melodies'* [1798]. *It was sometimes danced 'longways for as many as will' (as described in 'The Dancing Master'), but more frequently by one person.'*

John Playford first published *The Dancing Master* in 1651, with several successive editions up until 1728, and his description of the *Cheshire Round* is, as Dr Rimbault says, of a simple longways dance – where the couples dancing form two lines facing each other. He unfortunately gives no indication as to how the solo dance proceeds. My own feeling is that it was probably an undefined sequence of steps, leaps, and capers entirely dependent on the individual performer's preference and repertoire.

## 8. Cheshire Lads Are Chief of Men

Thy sons, old Cheshire, I will sing,
Dear county, long for heroes fam'd;
To England's foe a deadly sting,
Those foes their valour ever tam'd.
Europe – the world – all will maintain
Old Cheshire lads are chief of men.

Oft in the early days of yore,
When Rome's dread legions bore the sway;
Thy stream, oh Dee, flow'd red with gore,
While virtue did her charms display.
Rome's legions all, astonished then,
Own'd Cheshire lads were chief of men.

In Edward's or great Harry's days,
In Coeur de Lion's martial train;
Cheshire's sons' deeds did brightly blaze,
Then did immortal glory gain.
On Agincourt or Cressy's [sic] plain
Old Cheshire lads were chief of men.

Like their forefathers, greatly brave,
Old England's good each bosom warms;
From foes their country thus to save,
Their valiant sons are roused to arms.
Brave as their sires, they'll prove again,
Old Cheshire lads are chief of men.

From their beloved Deva's banks,
To Severn's side the heroes come;
Fir'd by warm zeal in martial ranks,
For war they leave a placid home.
Resolv'd that honour to maintain,
That Cheshire lads are chief of men.

Secure shall stand the Queen of Isles,
While freedom's banners are unfurl'd;
Secure in arms she grateful smiles,
And bids defiance to the world.
The lion rousing from its den,
Hails Cheshire lads the chief of men.

*Cheshire, chief of men* is an old saying and a typically modest Cheshire man's assessment of himself. An article in The Cheshire Sheaf of 1899 reports that *'In 'A brief view of the state of the Church of England', published 1653, the Bishop of Chester is referred to as having been 'Bishop of Man; but from thence he was translated to Chester, the Chiefe City of that Shire, that some call Chiefe of Men.''* Thomas Fuller in 1662 said of Cheshire *'Its gentry is remarkable on a four fold account - their numerousness, their antiquity, their loyalty, and their hospitality.'* The song is reported to have been addressed to the officers and men of the Western Cheshire Yeomen Cavalry by T Minshull and is dated November 1805. The *Dee* refers to the river, and *Deva* is the Roman name for Chester. It was supposedly sung to the tune of *Rule Britannia*, though I don't know how!

# 9. The Cheshire Man

A Cheshire man went o'er to Spain to trade in merchandise,
And when he'd come across the main a Spaniard there him spies.
'Now Cheshire man' quoth he, 'Look here, these fruits and spices fine
Our country yields these twice a year; thou hast not such in thine,
O - oh! Thou hast not such in thine.'

The Cheshire man soon sought the hold and brought a Cheshire cheese,
'Now Spanish Don' quoth he, 'See here, thou hast not such as these.
Your land produces twice a year fruits and spice you say,
But such as in my hand I bear, our land yields twice a day,
Aye! Our land yields twice a day.'

Now Cheshire men be strong in th'arm and likewise wick in th'ead,
They hoist their wench each Easter morn and then dance with lightsome tread.
So never let a Spaniard boast while Cheshire men abound
Lest they should teach him to his cost to dance a Cheshire Round,
Aye! To dance a Cheshire Round.

Another version of the *Cheshire Cheese*, this comes from Reg Holmes of Norley who I heard singing it in 1998. He learned it from three separate sources and then pieced them together into one complete song. In the last verse *'wick'* means quick or alive, as in a *wicken* hedge – one that is green and flourishing – and *'They hoist their wench each Easter morn'* is a reference to the tradition of *lifting* which is an old custom that caught my interest as soon as I saw it described as *'neither very pleasant nor particularly decent'*. A Manchester man writing in 1784 continues in more detail:

*'Lifting was originally designed to represent our Saviour's resurrection. The men lift the women on Easter Monday and the women lift the men on Tuesday. Sometimes, and perhaps more commonly, the lifters joined hands across each other's wrists, and thus made a sort of throne on which was placed the person to be lifted. He was then elevated two or three times, and sometimes carried for a little distance. His descent was much less ceremonious.'*

It would seem that anyone, on the payment of a small sum, could escape this indignity, but if the bribe was not forthcoming, then lifting proceeded. Not everyone, however, was keen to maintain such a fascinating custom, for in his book of local interest, *Cheshire Gleanings*, William Axon described what may well have been the last attempt at lifting before there was a public call to ban it as, like so many basically harmless pastimes, it had got out of hand and degenerated into rowdiness. He says:

*'The magistrates at Neston had a case before them at Easter of 1883 in which the old custom of lifting was in question. It would appear that on Easter Monday three men presented themselves at the house of the prosecutor, at Heswall, and told him that they had come to 'lift' his wife. The prosecutor told the defendant to go away or he would kick him out, as he would not allow anyone to take such liberties. The defendant, by way of excuse, informed the bench that he was only endeavouring to carry out an old Cheshire custom. The magistrates replied that he had acted most improperly, and must apologise and pay the costs.'*

No sense of tradition, some people.

## 10. The Cheshire Militia

Awhile brother soldiers attend;
Of the life that we lead I will sing:
We're militia men, called to defend
The cause of our country and king.
From the plains of lov'd Cheshire we come
O'er England we wander away;
We follow the beat of the drum,
And as ordered we love to obey.

Chorus: *For Cheshire men are still the same*
*Their fathers were, loyal and bold;*
*Chief of men they were called and the name*
*May we long be deserving to hold.*

If England but breathes the same soul
Which of old called her sons to the field
When they sought haughty France to control,
Again to our arms she must yield
We remember the name that we bear,
What our fathers have been in their day;
When they march'd against France, what they were
Let Cressy and Agincourt say!

With sense of our duty, like theirs,
May we still their example pursue;
And may Cheshire, as years follow years,
Possess hearts as honest and true.
To UNION then fill the glass high,
Victorious we long will remain;
To conquest or death we will fly,
Our King and our Laws to maintain.

This is believed to have been composed for the men of the Cheshire Militia by Lord Thomas Stanley (1766 - 1850). He was a major in the Militia before becoming the first Lord Stanley of Alderley in 1839. The song, written in September 1797, was printed and given away to soldiers, presumably to boost their morale and sense of loyalty.

## 11. Cheshire Regiment

(To the tune of *Lilli Marlene*)

There's a little song the Eighth Army used to hear
In a lonely desert romantic sweet and clear
Over the air it softly came, each night again
That sweet refrain
With you Lilli Marlene, with you Lilli Marlene

The Cheshire's had machine guns and they used them too
The DLI were infantry and they knew it too
We gave them support all around
In the air, and on the ground
With 'A' company leading to the foe

We were in the Mareth Line and did we know it too
Half a million rounds we fired just to see it through
Then on to Wadi Akerket, where Jerry made
His bold retreat

Now the battle's over 'The Two's' have gone to rest
They were the boys that always did their best
At the present morale is high, We know not why
But it's so high
Maybe we're bound for Blighty, maybe we're Blighty bound

*Lili Marlene*, written by Hans Leip and Norbert Shultze, was recorded by Lale Anderson just before the outbreak of World War II. When it was broadcast to the German Afrika Korps in 1941, British soldiers of the Eighth Army also listened in and the song became a huge success. The official English words were eventually written in 1944 by Tommy Connor and the tune was used to carry a wide range of soldiers' songs (most famously *The D-Day Dodgers*). This Cheshire Regiment version was collected from Jim Buckley, of Moulton, near Northwich. The *DLI* are the Durham Light Infantry and *The Two's* are the 2nd Battalion Cheshire Regiment (machine guns).

# 12. The Chester Garland
## In Four Parts

A merchant of London as may report,
He for a long time a fair lady did court,
At length by much courting this handsome lady,
Did promise this merchant his bride to be.
Of one thing this lady she was innocent,
To go his own factor this merchant was bent,
The ship was freighted, all things ready were,
In order to sail, but the wind was not fair.
So he to make sure of this lady bright
Was marry'd one morning before it was light,
And married they were, but the same day,
Tidings came to him the ship must away.
He said, 'My dear jewel, the thing it is so,
That I my own factor to India must go.
It will not be long e'er I shall return,
To your home in safety, dear do not mourn.'
So then he embark'd and away he did hie,
To be left alone, the lady did cry,
As he is gone from me I'll do what I can
To keep myself free from the scandal of man.
Then this noble lady with troubled mind,
She unto her chamber was thus confined,
Wherein I must leave her to sigh and complain,
And turn to the merchant who's gone o'er the main.
He sailed in to Russia whereas we find,
His ship was laden with traffick so fine.
Then to come to London his course he did steer
And what happened to him you quickly shall hear.
Upon the wide ocean a storm did arise
In which gloomy clouds did darken the skies.
The winds did blow, and the storms did roar,
Which drove them almost to the Irish shore.
For several hours by the waves they were tossed
Expecting each moment their lives to be lost,
In the midst of their danger, one did contrive
To alter their course, and at Chester arrive.
This thing was soon noised abroad in the town
And many shopkeepers to this ship came down,
One bought the whole cargo, the money, 'tis said,
To this London merchant in a few days was paid.
One day at a tavern these dealers we find,
Staid several hours in drinking of wine,
At length the shopkeeper said, 'Shall we go
And get us a miss?' The merchant said 'No.'
'Sir, with such a lady I fairly did wed,
And never had time to enjoy her bed,
A woman whose body no man ever knew,
Then to such a wife I will be chaste and true.'
The shopkeeper said, 'Your conceit is strong,
To think any woman could tarry so long
To wait for a husband. I'll lay if you dare,

That I can defile your chaste lady so fair.'
To which the merchant said, 'Sure I am free,
To lay ship and money on her chastity.'
Then before witness the thing was agreed,
And the shopkeeper to London came with speed.

He went to a tavern, and there did presume
To call for a bottle of wine and a room.
'Twas a widow woman who then lived there,
For the sake of the money, the wife did ensnare,
He asked if she knew such a one? The reply
Was 'Yes sir, and she liveth hard by.'
He said 'Fifty guineas I'll give you straightway
If into chamber you will me convey.'
Her answer was to him as I am alive,
'A way to get you there I soon will contrive.'
She went to this lady, and said 'It is so,
To my dying father this night I must go.
My jewels and plate and other things brave
Lie locked in a chest, which by me I have.
This night in your chamber pray let them lie here,
Tomorrow I'll fetch them, you need not to fear.'
This lady, not knowing her wicked design
Gave leave to bring it, at night we find
This vile, subtle bawd to compleat the jest
Had him conveyed when locked in the chest.
This lady she used to keep a great light
To burn in her chamber, always in the night,
And as this lady was in a deep sleep
The shopkeeper out of his chest did creep.
When he came to the bed, like one in amaze,
He on this lady did stand and gaze,
And on her right breast he espied a mole
Which for sometime he did stand and behold.
Likewise on the table he chanced to spy
A girdle and watch that on it did lie,
On her girdle and watch her name was placed,
Which things in his pocket he put up in haste.
Saying, 'These tokens my wager will gain,
And to disturb her I now must refrain',
Then into the chest he went and lay
Until the next morning he was fetched away.
So then for West Chester he did repair,
And with a good horse he soon came there
Crying to the merchant, 'The wager I've won
And if I mistake not, thou art undone.
Upon her right breast there is a mole grown
Which you in long courting have seen I suppose,
Sir, there is a girdle and a watch likewise,
Therefore you may see I tell you no lies.'
To see this the merchant wept bitterly,
And said 'Wicked strumpet thou hast ruined me.
For to be undone thus makes my heart ache
Now for a subsistence what course can I take.'
To hear his moan, some merchants being there,

Said to him 'Brother, do not despair,
Since you are ruined by a vile woman,
We'll make a man of you once more if we can.'
So among them they raised two hundred pounds,
And set him up shopkeeper in Chester town,
But Satan was busy, and to stir up strife
He tempted this merchant to kill his wife.

**H**e then kept a servant, whose name was John,
He then sent a letter to her by his man.
These words were in it 'At Chester I be
With all expedition dear wife come unto me.'
Perusing the letter she said with a smile
'My dear I'll be with you in a short while.'
Next day with this young man away she went,
Of these ill designs she was innocent.
Riding through a wood to make her his prey
He with a pen knife did turn and did say
'Come lady alight from your horse presently
For it is ordered here you must die.'
To hear these expressions she cried out amain,
'Young man wherefore is it I must be slain.'
His answer was 'For playing the whore
The man that defiled you, I knew before.'
She said 'If I must die, I'll take it on my death
No man ever knew me since I drew breath.'
He said 'These excuses never will do,
My master sent me to murder you.
He charged me to bring your clothes and heart,
Then I'll not prove false to him for my part.'
Thus as she stood trembling and for life did cry,
By providence a hog did chance to come by.
She said 'Save my life and kill that swine,
And take the heart, he'll think it's mine.
Likewise take these my clothes also
And give me yours, then a-wandering I'll go.'
For to save her life then he thought good
And the thing desired was done in the wood.
He went home and said 'Sir to finish the strife
Here are the clothes and heart of your wife.'
To see this the merchant did blush
And into the fire the heart did push,
Crying 'There's the heart of a strumpet again
Who has been my ruin and fed me with pain.'
Thus he in vile manner this heart did greet,
By which we might see that revenge is sweet,
But now I will leave him mistaken and hear
What course of life this lady did steer.

**D**rest in mans apparel she wandered away.
But as she was going through a town one day
She went to a gentleman's door it is said,
And begged heartily for a morsel of bread.
This man came forth and looked her in the face,
And said 'Young man it is a disgrace

For to go a begging, art thou willing said he
To serve such a master as now I may be?'
Her answer was 'Yes, and thank you beside'
'Come in and sit down' the master replied,
'And soon I will put better clothes on your back,
Be but a good servant thou nothing shall lack.'
This man so loved her that in a short space
He got her a commission for a Captain's place,
Then she with great courage to Flanders went o'er
And was in the battle where cannons do roar.
Summer being ended, both she and her men,
All that were alive, came to England again;
For winter quarters it was ordered so
That she and her men to West Chester must go,
Where walking the streets one night this lady
Looked into the shop and her husband did see.
For to think on his actions that were so base
Her heart was disturbed and moved from its place.
Dressed like a Commander to him she did go
And said unto him 'Sir, do you know
Such a man in the town? Tell me if you can.'
His answer was 'Sir, I am the man.'
'Sir, did you not marry with such a lady,
A noble knight's daughter, pray where is she?'
'Yes I married her' the merchant replied
'But three years ago she sickened and died.'
Then unto a Justice of Peace she retired
And told him the matter which things he admired,
He sent for her husband and the young man in haste,
With the villain that was locked in the chest.
But first he examined this lady's husband
But he with blushes looked very wan
And thinking his lady she had been dead
With fear his teeth gnashed in his head.
The justice said 'Young man for thee
Did'st thou kill this man's wife? Tell unto me.'
He said 'Sir I was sent this lady to kill
Unto her through mercy I shewed her no ill.
My master charged me to bring him her heart
But he was mistaken that time for his part
For 'twas a hog's heart I brought him to show
And I hope she is living, but where I don't know.'
Dressed in man's apparel she said to him 'John,
I am the young lady though dressed like a man.'
To hear that the merchant began to sweat
And looked like a woodcock caught in a net.
And then the shopkeeper was called in place
Who on this fair lady brought sorrow apace,
He being examined, was found guilty
And ordered to stand in the pillory.
Nay, this was not all, he was commanded to pay
Forty thousand pounds to the merchant next day;
Which sum was produced with great discontent
And straight to a prison he quickly was sent.
Saying 'I am ruined by playing the cheat

And shall be exposed to shame in the street.'
To prevent all scandal he took a penknife
And stabbed himself which ended his life.
And now this merchant and lady do dwell
Together in love and agree very well;
And as for the young man who pitied her moan
This lady loves him as a child of her own.

This rather long and complex story, proving that evildoers will get their comeuppance and good shall receive its rewards, is, perhaps, not so much a ballad as a soap opera and is from a broadside printed and sold by J Pitts, of Seven Dials. A broadside was simply a printed sheet of paper with the words of a song sold for a small amount of money. The material was sometimes traditional but often specially written and as A .L Lloyd, *Folk Song In England*, says:

*'In early days in country inns song-sheets were pasted up on fireplace surrounds and high bench-ends for the benefit of carters, ploughmen and others, and Walton the angler gives us an idyllic picture of the alehouse, 'lavender in the window and twenty ballads stuck about the wall.' Milkmaids would paper the walls of byres and dairies with broadsides, and learn off the ballads as they milked and churned, until the next coat of whitewash made ground for a new batch of lyrics.'*

In the broadside version of *The Contented Miller* [see *The Miller of the Dee*]:

*He cheerfully whistles, regardless of care,*
*Or sings the last ballad he bought at the fair.*

Lloyd also notes that in poor districts it was not unusual for more than one family to club together to buy a penny ballad sheet. The Pitts family together with their great rival James Catnach, both of Seven Dials, London, were probably the nineteenth century's most prolific producers of what was effectively the pulp fiction of its day.

# 13. Colin and Phoebe

"Well met my dearest Phoebe, Oh! Why in such haste?
Thro' the woods and the meadows all day have I chased,
In the search of my fair one, who does me disdain!
But I hope you'll reward me for all my long pain.
But I hope you'll reward me for all my long pain."

"Go, go boldest Colin, how dare you be seen,
With a virgin like me that is scarcely sixteen?
To be seen all alone with a man, I'm afraid,
This world will soon call me no longer a maid.
This world will soon call me no longer a maid."

"Never mind what the world says, it shall all prove a lie
We are not alone, there's a cottage hard by;
Let them judge of our actions, be cheerful, my dear,
For no harm is intended to my Phoebe, I swear.
For no harm is intended to my Phoebe, I swear."

"Go, go boldest Colin, you shall say what you will,
You may lie, swear, or flatter, and try your best skill;
But before I'll be conquer'd I'd have you to know,

I'll first die a virgin, so pray let me go.
I'll first die a virgin, so pray let me go."

"O, Phoebe, my charmer! Such thoughts I ne'er had,
I came for to see if to-morrow you'd wed;
But since you so slight me, I'll bid you adieu,
I'll go seek some other girl kinder than you.
I'll go seek some other girl kinder than you."

"Stay, stay, dearest Colin, a few moments stay,
I will venture to wed if you mean what you say;
Let to-morrow first come, love, in church you will find
That the lass you thought cruel will always prove kind.
That the lass you thought cruel will always prove kind."

According to Frank Kidson (1855 – 1926), who devoted most of his life to the collection and study of British song and dance music:

> *"'Colin and Phoebe' used to be sung in Yorkshire, and on the Lancashire and Cheshire borders, in the old fashioned style. It being 'a dialogue', a male and female singer took the respective parts, one as Colin and the other as Phoebe, and put as much archness and tenderness into their performance as the part warranted."*

This version was remembered by Mrs Holt as being sung in Stockport around 1840.

The song appears in broadside form as *Colin and Phebe* [sic] and *Corydon and Phillis* while Kidson goes on to mention that he believes himself to have discovered the original version as *Corydon and Phæbe* in a folio musical publication printed in 1755.

# 14. The Congleton Bear

You young men of Cheshire I'd have you to beware
Of the people and the pleasures of Congleton Fair;
In Congleton Bear Town where money for to save,
The Bible itself for a new bear they gave.

Chorus: *Congleton rare, Congleton rare,*
*They sold the church bible to buy a new bear.*

A new bible was wanted, the old book was done;
All the people agreed to subscribe to the sum.
At length they collected the money required,
To the joy of the parson, the clerk and the choir.

But the old bear decided it was time for a change,
And the week before the wakes was due he died of the mange.
A new bear was needed, nobody could deny;
The thought of the wakes was unbearably nigh.

When somebody whispered: 'The old book will do,
It's lasted us now for a good year or two;
With the parson's collection we'll buy a new bear.'
All the people agreed this decision was fair.

The parson preached daily of Congleton's shame,
The clerk wrote it down, the choir sang this refrain:
In Congleton Bear Town where money for to save,
The Bible itself for a new bear they gave.

*Congleton rare, Congleton rare, Sold the bible, to pay for a bear* was an old saying used to taunt the inhabitants of this fair town. Written here in song by Pete Coe, the story goes that in 1622 the church bible was so worn that the people of Congleton decided to have a collection to buy another. Unfortunately at the same time the town bear died and the keeper, applying to the corporation for funds to replace it, was granted the bible money for this purpose as the town wakes were imminent and they couldn't possibly contemplate such an event without a bear. The immense popularity of the 'sport' was such that they decided that the old bible could be used for a little bit longer and that replacing the bear constituted a far more pressing problem.

The wakes (usually referred to in the plural) were a time for feasting, celebration and general festivities. Each town and village had its own particular time of year for this, which was usually decided by the feast day of the saint to whom the local church was dedicated. Apart from bearing rushes to floor the church, there were many other sports, competitions and various amusements that could, in some cases, continue for several days. George Ormerod describes the annual wake as *'the most lively and picturesque, and the best known of these village customs.'* He goes on to say:

> *'All kind of country amusements go forward, bear and bull baits, donkey and smock races, cudgel play, grinning through horse collars, climbing soaped poles, and pulling at the soaped neck of a goose on a horse at speed.'*

Not all who witnessed these festivities took pleasure from them, as was the case with Mr John Bruen who William Axon (*Cheshire Gleanings*, 1884) refers to as a typical Puritan, and one who had *'a great horror of wakes and rush bearings.'* In an effort to avoid *'all riot and excess of eating and drinking, dalliance and dancing, sporting and gaming, and other abominable impieties and idolatries'* he invited the best preachers in the diocese to preach for the best part of the three days of Tarvin wakes. This he did *'so as the pipers, and fiddlers, and bearwards, and players, and gamesters had no time left for their varieties.'*

Talk about a party pooper!

# 15. The Curst Fisherman

Two fishermen loved Bessy Blake
A comely maid was she
Her parent's cot was at Hoylake
Not far from Hilbre

Two fishermen loved Bessy Blake,
Each other hated sore;
Their names John Stone and William Lake;
It was John that she favoured more.

A wild storm swept the Cheshire shore
While John was on the deep;
His boat, alas; it was seen no more,
Which made poor Bessy weep.

Early next morn, Will Lake he rose
And the waste of sand he sought;
Till landwards a sight that his life blood froze
The flowing billows brought.

For his rivals corpse lay stark and stare,
Swathed in slimy weed.
One hand still clasped a lock of hair,
Grasped in his utmost need.

When he saw that it was Bessy's hair
He spurned him as he lay,
And watched until the tide ebbed again
And washed the corpse away.

But a shrimper by an old wreck sat,
And from his hiding place
He viewed this deed, and then he told
Of this young man's disgrace.

For shame on a fisherman who leaves
A corpse the hoarse waves sport;
Whose winding-sheet the seawrack weaves,
And wild gulls scream the mort.

No peace had William from that hour,
Within, without the door;
That corpse's face on him would glower
Now and for evermore.

By Bessy scorned, for she'd been told
Who had her dead lover spurned.
Avoided by the young and old,
Despised where'er he turned.

By night, by day, at eve, at morn,
His rival's features sad
Gazed on him with that stare forlorn;
Till he finally went mad!

This song, subtitled *A Tale of the Wirral*, is from Egerton Leigh's *Ballads and Legends of Cheshire* (1867), where he names himself as contributor. The Wirral peninsula, once described as *'A piece of land between the seas behind Chester'*, was, up until the fourteenth century, a large forested area and is referred to in *Sir Gawayn and the Green Knight* as: *'The wilderness of Wyrale: few lived there who loved with a good heart either God or man'*, or as the local saying would have it: *'From Blacon Point to Hilbree, a squirrel may leap from tree to tree.'* It was also an area where there was much superstition relating to the sea. Some of it grew from the relative remoteness of the area, and some was possibly a smokescreen for the notorious wrecking activities when, in bad weather, the more unscrupulous inhabitants of the peninsula would use lights to guide ships onto the rocks and then rob them of their cargo. On parts of the coast some held the belief that once the sea had claimed a soul, it must be allowed to keep it, while others took the view that if you were to find a dead body washed up by the sea, it was your duty to make sure that it received a Christian burial. If you failed, then you would be haunted by the soul of the unfortunate victim for the rest of your days.

# 16. The Devil and the Monk

Come lords and ladies of high degree
And I'll tell you a tale that was whispered to me
How in Vale Royal a friar did chance
To take on the devil and lead him a dance.
The monks were asleep and the moon it shone clear
As the devil was flying o'er fair Delamere
The friar was dreaming of taking his fill
Of venison pasties and flagons of ale

The friar awoke with a terrible dread
For the devil was sat at the end of his bed
'Oh friar,' said he 'you can soon have your fill
If I can be witness to this your last will.'
He took out a scroll and in letters of fire
Shone forth the last will of Francis the friar
The monk read aloud what the devil did hold
And this was the bargain as I have been told.

'I give and bequeath all the goods that I have
To those who would carry my corpse to the grave
And when he has done all I ask him to do
Then my soul to the undersigned witness may go.'

The monk very soon put his name on the line
And the devil as witness did willingly sign
The papers all done, 'And now,' said the friar
'As part of this bargain three things I require.'

'First, venison pasties till appetite fail,
The second unlimited hogsheads of ale.
The third, on yonder Merton Sands,
You must find me and twine me a dozen hay bands.'
The devil sought grass by the light of the moon,
And the devil he searched in the sunshine of noon.
The devil he wandered from Mersey to Dee,
But on Merton Sands never a band twisted he.

The friar he sat on his cushion of state
Good ale he quaffed down and fine venison ate
Though all of his monks in good living did revel
He never again would say done to the devil.
But still every year stout yeomen are found
Who on Merton Sands will fallow the ground,
Where never a blade of green grass shall remain
Lest the devil comes back to Vale Royal again.

Another local story gleaned from Egerton Leigh's *Ballads and Legends of Cheshire* (1867), this time contributed by Rev J Sedgwick and described as *A Legend of Merton Sands*. According to Egerton Leigh, Merton Sands were a mile or so from Over, near Winsford, but Mr G H Longrigg in his book *Legends of the Dee* (1901), suggests that most evidence points to their being at Moreton on the Wirral where he says *'the mere has long since been drained, but the broad sands still stretch the whole length of the coast between Mersey and Dee.'* He also quotes another old song, which runs:

*'Many have told of the Monks of old*
*What a saintly race they were:*
*But 'tis most true, a merrier crew*
*Could scarce be found elsewhere,*
*For they sang and laughed,*
*And the rich wine quaffed,*
*And lived on the daintiest fare.*

*'And the Abbot meek, with his form so sleek,*
*Was heartiest of them all;*
*And would take his place, with a smiling face,*
*When the Refectory bell would call.*
*And they sang and laughed,*
*And the rich wine quaffed,*
*Till they shook the oden Hall'*

Wherever the sands were, legend has it that there was a festive gathering every year for the purpose of ploughing them. Nothing ever grew there and the ploughing was to make sure that nothing ever did – just in case the devil ever came back to claim the friar's soul. A *hogshead* is a large cask with a capacity of 52½ imperial gallons.

# 17. The Farmer's Boy

The sun had set behind yond hill
Across the dreary moor,
When weary and lame a boy there came
Up to the farmer's door.
'Say, can you tell me where'er there be
One that would employ
For to plough and sow, to reap and to mow,
And to be a farmer's boy,
And to be a farmer's boy.'

'My father is dead, and mother is left
With five children, great and small;
And what is worse for mother still,
I'm the oldest of them all.
Though little I'll work as hard as a Turk,
If you'll give me employ,
To plough and sow, and reap and mow
And be a farmer's boy,
And be a farmer's boy.

'And if that you won't me employ,
One favour I've to ask –
Will you shelter me, till break of day,
From this cold winter's blast?
At break of day, I'll trudge away
Elsewhere to seek employ
To plough and sow, and reap and mow

And be a farmer's boy,
And be a farmer's boy.'

'Come try the lad,' the mistress said,
'Let him no further seek;'
'O, do, dear father!' the daughter cried,
While tears ran down her cheek;
'He'd work if he could, so 'tis hard to want food,
and wander for employ;
don't turn him away, but let him stay,
And be a farmer's boy,
And be a farmer's boy.'

And when the lad became a man,
The good old farmer died,
And left the lad the farm he had,
And his daughter for his bride.
The lad that was, the farm now has,
Oft smiles, and thinks with joy,
Of the lucky day he came that way,
To be a farmer's boy,
To be a farmer's boy.

From the singing of Ernest Collins of Altrincham, recorded by Mike Yates in 1975. Ernest, unfortunately, only sang the first verse and the rest of the story has been filled out from a version collected on the borders of Lancashire and Yorkshire. The slight variation in his tune, however, may take one or two people familiar with the song by surprise – it certainly did me – though Frank Kidson in *Traditional Tunes* includes three airs for the song that differ greatly. The original words to the most widely used tune would appear to be a patriotic anthem called *Ye Sons of Albion* which runs:

*Ye sons of Albion, rise to arms,*
*And meet the haughty band;*
*They threaten us with war's alarms,*
*And ruin to our land.*
*But let no rebel Frenchman sans-culottes,*
*Nor the dupes of tyranny boast*
*To conquer the English, the Irish, and the Scots,*
*Or to land upon our coast, or to land upon our coast.*

Although *The Farmer's Boy* was a popular song in all corners of the country, especially among agricultural workers in the late nineteenth century, there is a belief among many that the original 'boy made good' was from Cheshire. In *The Cheshire Round* (Vol 1, No 5, 1966, p136) Geoffrey Nulty tells the story of how the Reverend Thomas Smith came to the village of Little Leigh, near Northwich, looking for work.

*'He called at Heath House Farm, was given a job, and in time married the farmer's daughter just as the song relates. Later he became a Baptist minister and he is buried in the graveyard of the chapel.'*

That's the story anyway.

# 18. Froggie

There was an old frog and he lived in a well,
*Ding, Dang, Dong, go the wedding bells,*
And a pretty little mouse lived in a mill,
*Ding, Dang, Dong, go the wedding bells.*

Chorus: *Here's to Cheshire, here's to the cheese,*
*Here's to the pears and the apple trees,*
*And here's to the lovely strawberries,*
*Ding, Dang, Dong, go the wedding bells.*

Froggie went a-courting and he did ride,
*Ding, Dang, Dong go the wedding bells,*
Now Missie Mouse you must decide,
*Ding, Dang, Dong go the wedding bells,*
I am rich and I am brave,
*Ding, Dang, Dong go the wedding bells,*
What better husband could you have?
*Ding, Dang, Dong go the wedding bells.*

Oh I'd never take your word for that,
You'll have to satisfy Uncle Rat.
Says Uncle Rat 'I'm much afraid,
If you don't take Froggie you'll die an old maid.'

The knot was tied secure and fast,
She's off her uncle's hands at last.
Open the oysters, spill champagne,
Never will there be such a feast again.

Tune up the fiddles, lets have a square,
Top couple must be the happy pair.
But as they were going it hot and strong,
The good grey cat came prowling along.

She jumped through the window right out of the yard,
Didn't bring no invitation card.
Uncle Rat like a hero stood,
Pussie wet her whiskers in his blood.

Little Missie Mouse made a dive for a crack,
Puss made a pounce and broke her back.
But where was the valiant frog this while?
He just about broke the four-minute mile.

He came to the brook and he didn't stop to look,
The old drake nabbed him in his fluke.
So that was the end of both him and her,
Won't be no tadpoles covered with fur.

This song, made by Leslie Haworth (he strongly believed that songs were 'made' rather than written as this gave greater allowance for other people's interpretation), has become something of a Cheshire anthem having been sung all over the world. Leslie was a monumental figure in the sphere of local history and culture and, apart from his fine singing and song writing, he also played a significant role in the formation of the Manley Morris Dancers.

In 1934 his sister, Dorothea Haworth, was organising the country dances in Manley village and had received a number of requests for displays at fêtes, shows, etc. and enquiries resulted in Bob McDermott from the Royton dancers coming to Manley on a regular basis to train a team. He remained with them, continuing to lead the dancers, and in 1935 they recruited Caleb Walker, then a waggoner on a Manley farm and a fine concertina player, as lead musician. The team gave a few performances between 1935 and 1939 but at that time most of the team were required for hand milking on Saturday afternoons and could rarely be excused. The war, unfortunately, put an end to the dancing and it was not resumed for another ten years.

In 1950 he gathered a nucleus of dancers, largely made possible by the boys' team that was active before the war, along with stalwarts Arthur Webb, Albert Fletcher, Bob McDermott and Caleb Walker, who were all keen to carry on. Their first big post-war engagement was at the Hexham Festival in 1952 and in January 1953 they made their first appearance at the Royal Albert Hall. In June of the same year, in combination with the Loftus Sword Dancers, they won the International Trophy at the Llangollen International Eisteddfod gaining 98 points out of a possible 100 with fidelity to tradition being especially commented on. The team is still going strong with Leslie's son Colin (from whom I learned this song) still playing an active part and they remain, in my humble opinion, the best in the land.

# 19. The Glorious Sixth of May

Hark! down the Deva's wizard stream
The Eight bells pour their silver sound
The Eight bells pour their silver sound
Roused from a long a long prophetic dream
The River Goddess looks around
What sound is this, what thundring loud huzza
Thus wakes me on the sixth of May

His head sublime with turrets crown'd
Old Cestria's genius thus replies,
Oh Lady Deva, look around
With transport lift thy Aged eyes
To Egerton and Freedom and Freedom ever gay
We consecrate the sixth of May!

Lo! Where advance in lengthen'd train
Bright Honour's form and sacred Truth
Mark Independence upright mien
While modest worth points out the youth,
Then let thy banks re-echo to the lay
All hail the glorious sixth of May!

Since Edgar stern did proudly ride
His tributary Kings among,
No sight like this has grac'd thy tide
No theme so worthy of a song,
Strike then the Lyre and strains exalted play
To hail the glorious sixth of May!

Now may'st thou hope thro' deepen'd bed,
Where ocean meets thy soft embrace
The well-fraught bark shall oft be led,
The rising pile thy sides shall grace
While wealth shall Arts and Industry repay
And Commerce bless the sixth of May!

Well please'd the Goddess hears the strain
And thus replies, O Genius dear,
Long have I wish'd but wish'd in vain,
From thee, my son, such news to hear,
Now shall my waves in grateful murmurs say
Hail! Hail the Glorious sixth of May!

Go then my streams by art convey'd
Across Llangollen's beauteous vale
To infant Commerce lend your aid
Fill the Canal and bear the sail
Replenished banks and barges on their way
Shall smiling bless the sixth of May!

What, tho' that ancient house decline
Whose White spire decorate my shore
In emulative zeal to join
With us to tug the lab'ring oar,
Let Oulton's Walls and Cestria's Turrets gay
Still bless the glorious sixth of May!

According to Dr Bridge in his volume of Cheshire proverbs *'On May 6th, 1807, the City of Chester returned John Grey Egerton of Oulton Park as member of parliament and, for the first time, overthrew the house of Grosvenor which for nearly one hundred years had monopolised the representation. The effect was indescribable. A song was written and the saying and the song became a war-cry for the Independents and roused a state of feeling and excitement in the city such as we are unable to understand at the present day. Fathers taught their children this song and it was handed down from generation to generation.'* The music was written by Richard Taylor, a well known local musician who kept a music shop in Watergate Street, and the words were by 'A Freeman'. Mr Bridge, however claims to have had a contemporary manuscript attributing the words to a Mr J Jenkins, but he suggests that evidence also points to their being written by a Mr Richard Houghland. Dr Bridge describes this song by saying that *'Both words and music reflect the poor taste of the period.' 'Deva's wizard stream'* is a quotation from Milton *('nor yet where Deva spreads her wizard Stream')*, whose poem *Lycidas* was *'a lament for a friend drowned in his passage from Chester on the Irish seas, 1637'*, and the *'eight bells'* are those of St John's Church, near the river.

# 20. I'm Afraid I Shall Never Be Married

*The Bargain*

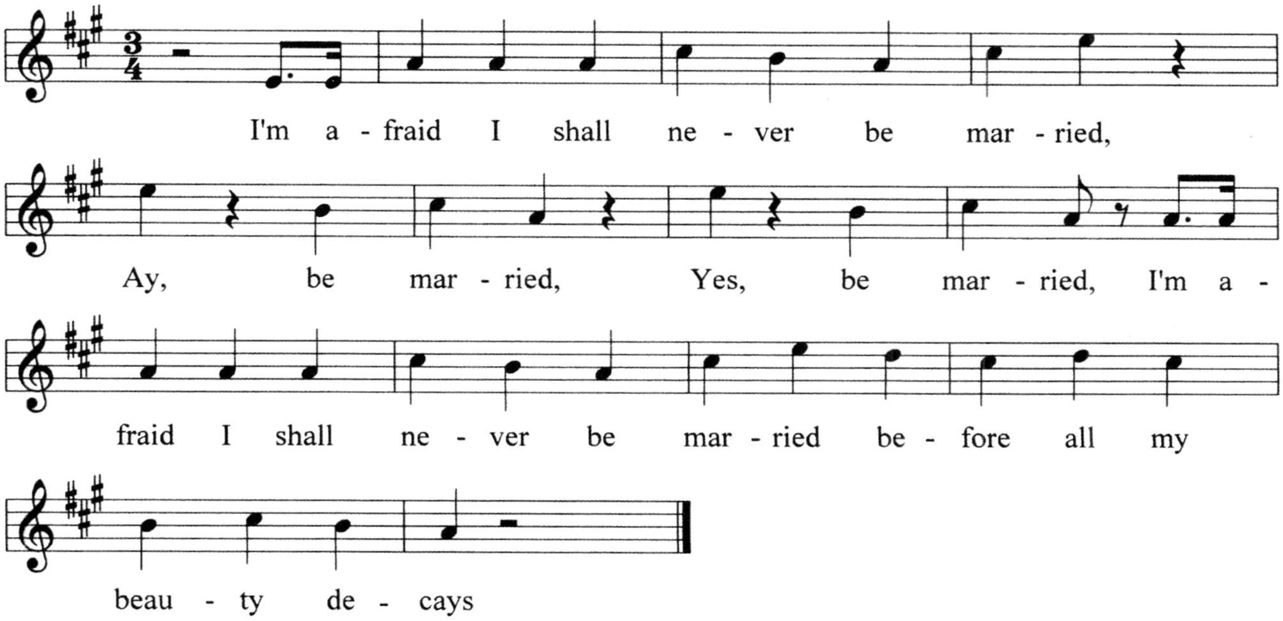


I'm afraid I shall never be married,
Ay, be married, yes, be married,
I'm afraid I shall never be married,
Before all my beauty decays

My shoes they are gone to be mended,
Mended, mended,
My shoes they are gone to be mended,
My petticoat to be dyed green

And shall I not then be a bargain,
A bargain, a bargain,
And shall I not then be a bargain
For someone to carry away!

They'll all be ready by Sunday,
Ay by Sunday, yes, by Sunday,
They'll all be ready by Sunday,
And I shall be fine as a queen.

Printed in the Manchester Guardian of 2nd August 1907, this was contributed 'L.G.' from Hazel Grove, near Stockport, who recalled it *'as we children used to sing it more that sixty years ago'* (i.e. around 1845). Of the four verses sent, though, only the first and last were included and verses 2 & 3 are from another version contributed to the *Journal of the English Folk Song Society* in 1929 by Anne Geddes Gilchrist. She noted the song from her mother who had learnt it as a young girl from an old blind Scots minister in Dumfriesshire around 1855. Miss Gilchrist explains *'She used as a young girl to go for long walks with him, and when either or both were beginning to flag, he would strike up the lively air and song as a marching-tune, to which they stepped out with renewed briskness.'*

## 21. John Lomas's Farewell

Good people all I pray attend
Unto these lines which here is penned;
A cruel murder I did commit,
And now I do repent of it.

I had a master very kind,
But my mistress on me did set her mind;
And she did teaze me night and day
To take his precious life away.

Soon unto her I did consent,
On murder I was fully bent,
For she told me in a little space
I should be happy in his place.

My master has some liquor got,
Not knowing of our wicked plot;
To bed he went, did sleep and snore,
Not thinking he should rise no more.

My mistress found he was asleep,
Then from her room did softly creep,
And she did come to my bed side,
"To kill him now's the time", she cried.

Three times I struck him on the head,
And thought he surely had been dead,
But he did spring out on the floor,
Which much surprised us, to be sure.

My mistress by me she did stand,
All with a razor in her hand,
"Take this", says she, "and end his life
And I will be your loving wife".

I cut his throat immediately
And out the crimson blood did fly,
All over me and on the floor,
The scene was awful, to be sure.

Then to my room I did return,
My conscience did like fuel burn,
My crime was of so deep a dye
That murder did for vengeance cry.

Immediately now as you see,
I was proved the murderer for to be;
For with his blood my shirt was dyed,
A truth that could not be denied.

To Chester Gaol then I was ta'en,
In heavy irons to remain,
In dismal cell so very strong,
Till the assizes came on.

When at the Bar I did appear,
The evidence it was so clear,
The jury all did "Guilty" cry
And I was soon condemned to die.

John Lomas now it is my name,
From Audlem Green in Cheshire came;
At twenty years old you see
I come to die on the fatal tree.

May young and old a warning take,
And think on my untimely fate!
Here you may see the offence and crime
For which I suffer in my prime.

John Lomas, servant to one George Morrey, was believed to be having an affair with his master's wife, Edith, and when George's body was found (in his bedroom with his throat cut) the evidence pointed to a conspiracy. Both John and Edith were charged with what was then called 'Petty Treason' – with George being head of the household, it would be expected that he should receive the same standards of loyalty from his wife and servant as any good subject would owe to the reigning monarch. John Lomas was hanged on August 24th 1812, and almost immediately his dismal tale in ballad form was being sold on the streets of Chester, this version being from a broadside printed by G Coman of Nantwich [see also *Rope Dance*]. Edith Morrey 'pleaded her belly' at the trial but, after the birth of a son, was finally hanged on April 23rd 1813.

The full title of the printed ballad is *The Sorrowful Lamentation, Confession and Last Farewell to the World of John Lomas* and is preceded, in typically dramatic style, by the following:

> **May my fate be a warning to sinful men, whereby they may forsake their evil ways, and search after righteousness. May the words of a dying man persuade them to this glorious effort, that they may be convinced of its necessity, in order to secure for themselves peace in this world, and everlasting felicity in the world to come. Happy would my end have been had I followed this conduct: shame and terror is my reward for departing from it.**

# 22. Joseph Baker

You sporting men of Chester, I'd have you all to hear
Of a man called Joseph Baker, who lived near Delamere.
He ran faster than the old red fox, and farther than the hound,
Of all the men who challenged him, no equal could be found.

He rose up every morning before the day was clear,
And through the shady forest he pursued the royal deer.
He chased the wind across the field, the mist right up the hill,
He raced the dust along the road, and the stream down to the mill.

Now sportsmen came from far and near to challenge Baker's speed;
At every race at every place, they swore to do that deed.
A tailor came from Frodsham, a soldier came from Hale,
A sailor came from Birkenhead, and a butcher came from Sale.

But he was never beaten until that fateful day,
When death at last defeated him and took his breath away.
And if you should watch on a winter's night, you'll see him running still,
As his ghost runs down from Kelsall church, right up to Helsby Hill.

Yes, if you should watch on a winter's night, you'll see him running still,
As his ghost runs down from Kelsall church, right up to Helsby Hill.

Joseph Baker was a Cheshire based long distance runner and this song, based on a broadside [see *The Navigator's New Victory*], was written by Pete Coe using a variant of *The Miller of the Dee* for the melody. Such feats of physical prowess were highly regarded and there are frequent reports of similar athletic achievements. There is, for example, the case of Joseph Edge, the 'Macclesfield

Pedestrian', who (in 1806 at the age of 62) is reported to have walked from Macclesfield to London in 49 hours and 20 minutes. There is also a note in the *Sporting Magazine* of 1792 which says that on 21st May of that year *'A very young boy, for a trifling wager, ran twice round the City Walls of Chester (three miles and a half) in 23 minutes; numerous spectators were present, who deemed it a very extraordinary pedestrian exploit, particularly as the youth was only 12 years of age.'*

# 23. The Keys of Heaven

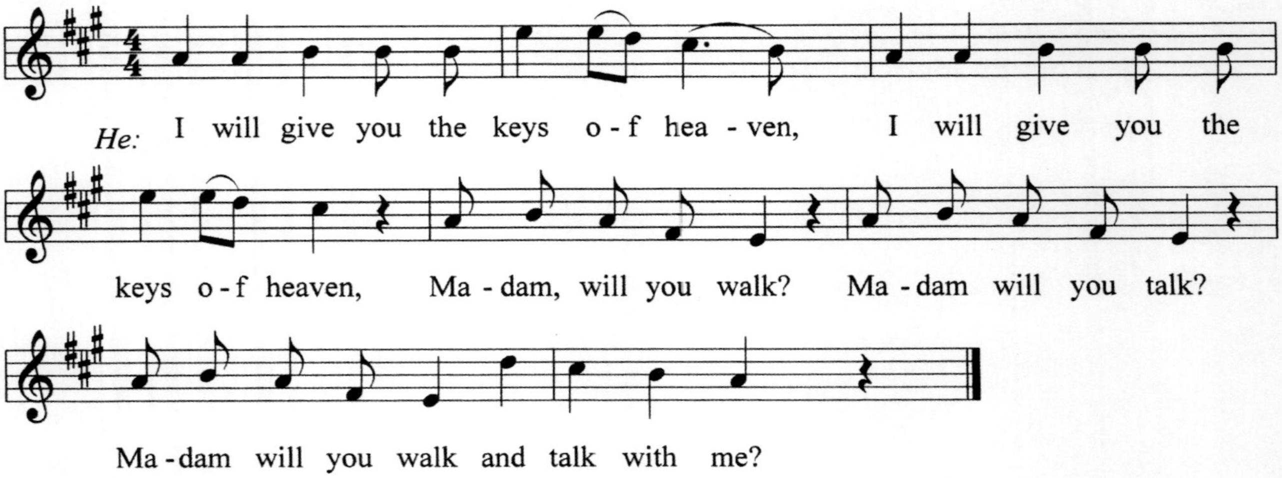


*He*: I will give you the keys of heaven,  
I will give you the keys of heaven,  
Madam will you walk? Madam will you talk?  
Madam will you walk and talk with me?

*She*: Though you give me the keys of heaven,  
Though you give me the keys of heaven,  
Yet I will not walk; no, I will not talk;  
No, I will not walk or talk with you.

*He*: I will give you a blue silk gown,  
To make you fine when you go to town.

*She*: Though you give me a blue silk gown,  
To make me fine when I go to town.

*He*: I will give you a coach and six,  
Six black horses as black as pitch.

*She*: Though you give me a coach and six,  
Six black horses as black as pitch.

*He*: I will give you the keys of my heart,  
And we will be married till death us do part.

*She*: Thou shalt give me the keys of thy heart,  
And we'll be married till death us do part;  
I will walk; I will talk;  
I will walk and talk with thee.

From *English County Songs* (1893) by Lucy Broadwood and J A Fuller Maitland, which states that *'the first two stanzas and the tune come from Cheshire, the other verses were forgotten, but are restored from an East country version.'* The song was collected by the Rev S Baring-Gould from the Rev F Partridge and can also be found in *Cheshire Notes and Queries* (1899).

In *Folk Songs From Somerset* Cecil Sharp also records a song entitled *The Keys of Heaven*, which begins:

*O Madam I will give to you the keys of Canterbury,*
*And all the bells in London shall ring to make us merry,*
*If you will be my joy, my sweet and only dear,*
*And walk along with me anywhere.*

# 24. The Lost Lady Found

It was down in a valley a young maiden did dwell,
She lived with her uncle as all knew full well;
'Twas down in the valley where violets were gay,
Three gypsies did betray her, three gypsies did betray her,
Three gypsies did betray her, and stole her away.

Long time she'd been missing and could not be found,
Her uncle he searched the country around,
Till he came to her Trustee between hope and fear,
The Trustee made answer, she had not been here.

The Trustee spoke up with courage so bold,
'I fear she has been lost for the sake of her gold,
So we'll have life for life, sir,' the Trustee did say,
'We shall send you to prison, and there you shall stay.'

There was a young squire that loved her so,
Oft-times to the school house together they did go;
'I'm afraid she is murdered, so great is my fear,
If I'd wings like a dove I would fly to my dear.'

He travell'd thro' England, thro' France, and thro' Spain,
Till he ventured his life on the watery main;

And he came to a house where he lodged for a night,
And in that same house was his own heart's delight.

When she saw him she knew him, and flew to his arms,
She told him her grief while he gazed on her charms;
'How came you to Dublin, my dearest?' said he.
'Three gypsies did betray me and stole me away.'

'Your uncle's in England, in prison does lie,
And for your sweet sake is condemned for to die.'
'Carry me to old England, my dearest,' she cried,
'One thousand I will give you, and will be your bride.'

When she came to old England her uncle to see,
The cart it was under the high gallows tree:
'Oh, pardon! Oh pardon! Oh pardon! I crave,
Don't you see I'm alive, your dear life to save?'

Then straight from the gallows they led him away,
The bells they did ring and the music did play!
Every house in the valley with mirth did resound,
As soon as they heard the 'Lost Lady' was found.

In Barrett's *English Folk-Songs* (1891) he records that *'This beautiful melody was sent from Cheshire'.* Although it would appear that this set of words is from the London area the song is worthy of inclusion for the tune alone. Versions of this tale abound throughout the country and songs known as *Gipsy Song*, *Three Gypsies Betrayed Her*, *The Lost Lady*, or *As Down In A Valley* will often turn up very similar stories.

# 25. The Marlers' Song

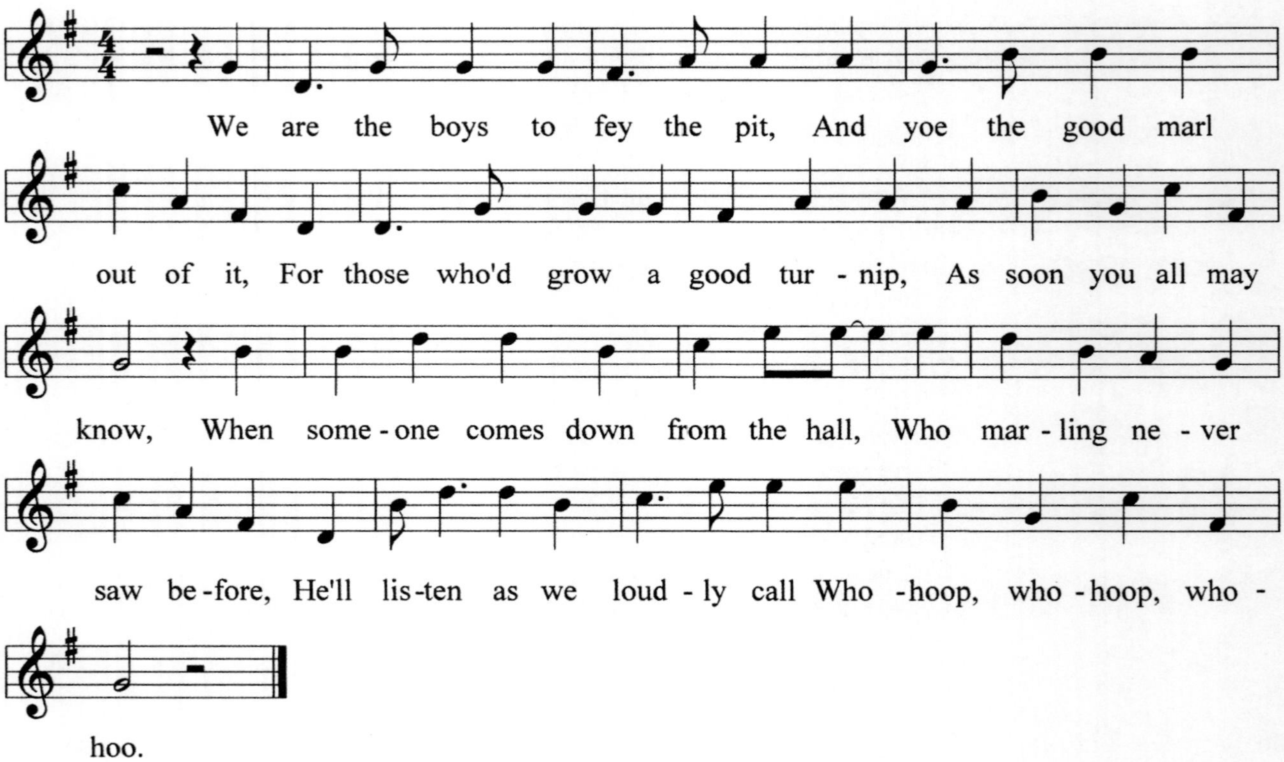


We are the boys to fey the pit,
And yoe the good marl out of it
For those who'd grow a good turnip,
As soon you all may know.
When someone comes down from the hall,
Who marling never saw before,
He'll listen as we loudly call
Who-hoop, who-hoop, who-hoo

But we must of one thing take heed,
Lest there's a slip at the marl head,
And then we'd all be crushed stark dead.
As soon you all may know.
But soon our lord will lorgesse take;
And then our thanks we'll rightly make,
And shout until our sides do ache.
Who-hoop, who-hoop, who-hoo

At the week's end we all will meet,
Where we know that the liquor's reet,
And there we'll drink into the neet.
As soon you all may know
When the pit is shut, the marler's law,
Is he we work for opes his door,
And gives to us of drinks galore,
Who-hoop, who-hoop, who-hoo

The marlers were itinerant labourers who worked in gangs and would travel around the county digging marl, a combination of clay and carbonate of lime, used as a fertiliser. Some tenants were bound by their lease to marl part of their farm annually and this helped give rise to the old saying *he who marls the sand, buys the land,* implying that such good farming practice would be sure to bring prosperity. The first process was to *'fey'* the pit, meaning to clear away the surface, usually sand, to get at the marl. To *'yoe'* was a local expression meaning to hew or cut with the edge of a spade, and the *'lord of the pit'*, the head marler of the gang, received any payment or *'lorgesse'* on behalf of the others. The *'marl head'* was the deepest part of the pit, which had an unfortunate tendency to collapse, and *'shutting the pit'* denoted the end of the gang's contracted work. Each gang had its own cry and when they received payment for their work they would gather round and shout this as loud as they could – hence the 'call' at the end of each verse. According to Ormerod (*History of Cheshire*, 1882): *'The same ceremony is repeated at the village ale-house, where they spend their acquisitions on Saturday, and the sound of the last prolonged shout, as it dies gradually away, may be heard for miles in a still summer's evening.'*

As for the efficacy of the substance, Ernest Collins (see *The Farmer's Boy*) recalls but one incident of marling which took place at Wincham when Brunner Mond were excavating a bore hole and in doing so removed a large quantity of marl. He recalls that his employer at the time instructed him and another man to take a horse and cart to collect the marl and spread it on the ground. This they did with the result that the land yielded, in Ernest's estimation anyway, *'twice the crop of oats after it.'*

## 26. May Song – Cheshire

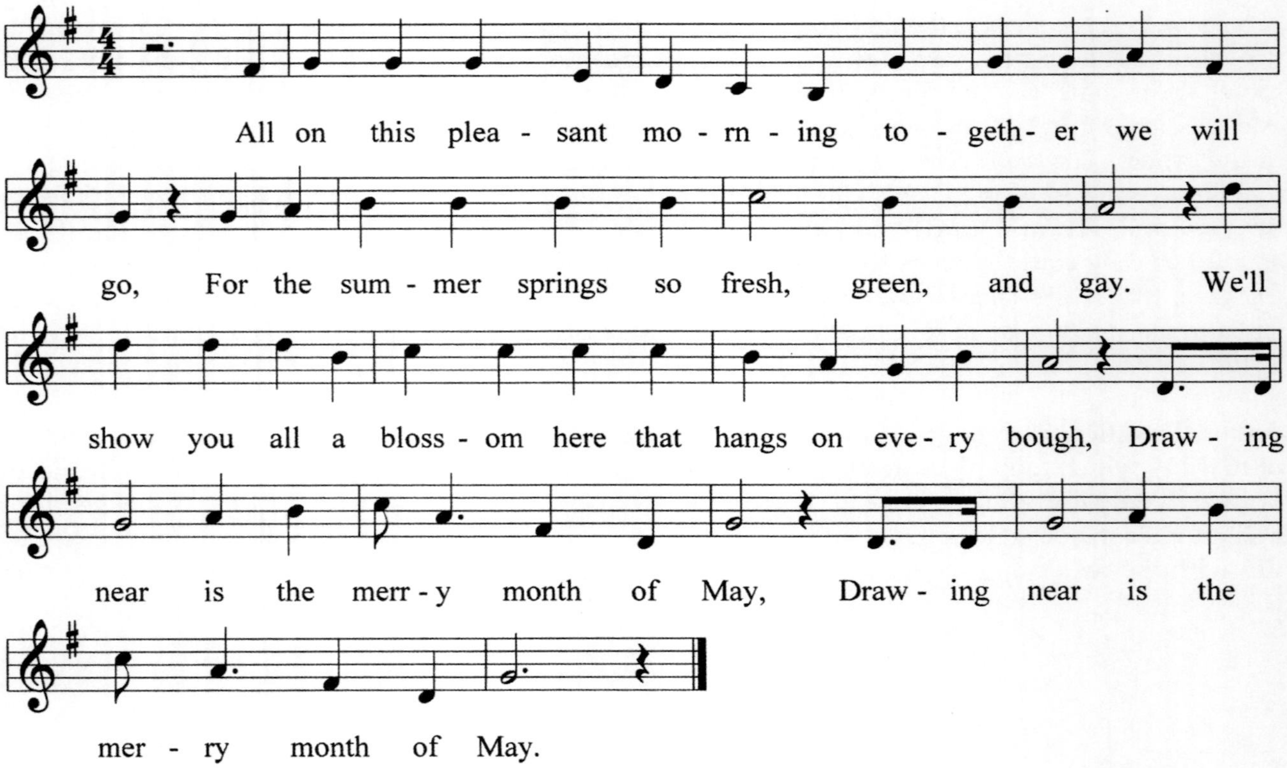


All on this pleasant morning together we will go
For the summer springs so fresh, green and gay
We'll show you all a blossom here that hangs on every bough
Drawing near is the merry month of May,
Drawing near is the merry month of May.

Rise up good master of this house, and kindly mistress too,
For the summer springs so fresh, green and gay.
We wish you best of health and wealth to last your days all through,
Drawing near is the merry month of May,
Drawing near is the merry month of May.

Rise up fair maiden of this house, put on your gown of silk,
For the summer springs so fresh, green and gay.
You are deserving of a man with forty cows to milk,
Drawing near is the merry month of May,
Drawing near is the merry month of May.

Rise up young masters of this house, put on your coats of blue,
For the summer springs so fresh, green and gay.
And to the sweethearts of your choice, we hope that you'll prove true,
Drawing near is the merry month of May,
Drawing near is the merry month of May.

Long may you live to prosper and happy may you be,
For the summer springs so fresh, green and gay.
And blessed in contentment to all eternity,

Drawing near is the merry month of May,
Drawing near is the merry month of May.

And now we're going to leave you in peace and plenty here,
For the summer springs so fresh, green and gay.
We'll come no more a May-singing until another year,
Drawing near is the merry month of May,
Drawing near is the merry month of May.

This version, from the singing of Reg Holmes of Norley, is one of many songs celebrating the first of May. Although it would appear that in some parts of the county at least the celebrations were to herald the approach of this special time of year and would end on the 30th April, other accounts relate activities confined to the day itself. Hilda Gamlin (*Memories of Birkenhead*, 1892) recalls:

> *'The day that ushered in the merry month of May was an ever memorable one in the forties,* [one assumes the 1840s] *for a miniature carnival brought together a large concourse of sight-seers.'*

She goes on to describe a scene which seemed to consist mostly of men dressed as women and a May Queen (who also appears to have been male).

*'Gigantic blue roses mingled with white, yellow and pink and an enormous bunch of many-hued ribbons dangled from the back of his head. Festoons of gaudy ribbons and flowers decorated the skirt.'*

This group danced through the town, accompanied by a small band consisting of a kettledrum, tin whistles and little rattles with small trays standing in for tambourines, until they reached the site of the Maypole. She continues:

*'On arriving at this point in Hamilton Street a collection was made from the lookers-on, and then there issued from the May ground the female element, who now took part in the show, their dresses pretty short, chemisette bodices, and the sleeves turned up, leaving the arms bare. The men faced the women, and they advanced towards each other in threes, forming into straight rows of nine in each line; then, with a step partly swaying, partly capering, they met and took partners, dancing off to the field, where the first who entered encircled the Maypole with his arm and swung round it, the rest following in like manner. Then all joined hands, and gambolled in an immense circle round the pole in true Old English style.'*

Reg also informs me that the fifth verse (*Long may you live to prosper etc.*) was sometimes recited at marriage ceremonies as a blessing for the bride and groom.

# 27. May Song – Mobberley

All on this pleasant morning together we will go;
For the summer springs so fresh, green, and gay;
We'll tell you of a blossom here that hangs on every bough;
Drawing near is the merry month of May.
Drawing near is the merry month of May.

Rise up the master of this house, you are the country's pride;
For the summer springs so fresh, green, and gay;
And turn unto your loving wife who lies down by your side;
Drawing near is the merry month of May.

Rise up the mistress of this house, with gold upon your breast;
For the summer springs so fresh, green, and gay;
And if your body be asleep we hope your soul's at rest;
Drawing near is the merry month of May.

Rise up the children of this house, so pretty and so fine;
For the summer springs so fresh, green, and gay;
And every hair upon your head like silver it should shine;
Drawing near is the merry month of May.

Rise up the young man of this house, put on your coat of blue;
For the summer springs so fresh, green, and gay;

And to the girl that you love best, we hope you will be true;
Drawing near is the merry month of May.

Rise up the fair maid of this house, put on your gown of silk;
For the summer springs so fresh, green, and gay;
You are deserving of a man with forty cows to milk;
Drawing near is the merry month of May.

So now we're going to leave you in peace and plenty here;
For the summer springs so fresh, green, and gay;
And we'll come no more a-May-singing until another year;
For to drive the cold winter away.

In *A Glossary of Some Words Used in the County of Chester*, 1886, Robert Holland describes hearing the May singers at Mobberley and records this song as being taken down from their singing around 1850. He went on to say that he never heard May singing anywhere else although he did not suppose that the practice of *'welcoming "the merry month" was confined to that locality.'* I think he was right there. I have found numerous versions of the May song from all corners of the county, often very similar to each other, showing that, at one time at least, the practice was indeed widespread. Christina Hole in *Traditions and Customs of Cheshire* (1937), says:

*'Perhaps the most popular of spring festivals was May-Day. In the old Celtic year it ranked as the beginning of summer, and a whole host of superstitions and customs have gathered round it. On 30th April the May-birchers went round decorating the houses according to their likes and dislikes, and the May carol was sung.'*

She continues:

*'At one time, the young people of the village used to go out into the woods at midnight to gather green branches and flowers for the garlands, a practice much disliked by the Puritans, who thought it led to immorality.'*

# 28. The Miller of the Dee

There was a jolly miller lived on the river Dee,
He worked and sang from morn til night, no lark more blithe than he;
And this the burden of his song forever used to be,
'I care for nobody, no not I, if nobody cares for me.'

The reason why he was so blithe he once did thus unfold,
'The bread I eat my hands have earned; I covet no man's gold;
I do not fear next quarterday; in debt to none I be,
I care for nobody, no not I, if nobody cares for me.'

'A coin or two I've in my purse to help a needy friend;
A little I can give the poor, and still have some to spend.
Though I may fail, yet I rejoice another's goodhap to see,
I care for nobody, no not I, if nobody cares for me.'

So let us his example take, and be from malice free;
Let everyone his neighbour serve as served he'd like to be;
And merrily push the can about, and drink and sing with glee,
If nobody cares a doit for us, then not a doit care we.

The words of this popular song were first printed in 1762 when they appeared in Arne's opera *Love In A Village* but it is likely that the song was and old one even then. Of the various versions this, supposed by the finder to be the original, was discovered in the mid-nineteenth century on the flyleaf of a volume of Dryden's poems, printed in 1716.

The Dee Mills, situated at the end of the Old Dee Bridge in Chester, had the sole right to grind the city's grain which proved a very profitable enterprise, and the Earl of Chester, by his Chamberlain and other officers, kept a Court at the mills to deal with cases of extortion by the millers, stealing of corn, and riotous behaviour by frequenters of the mills. The mills' effective monopoly and its prime location meant that it also commanded the highest rents in the city, giving rise to the old saying *If thou hadst the rent of Dee Mills, thou wouldst spend it,* meaning the height of extravagance. In 1284 the mills were rented at £200 per annum but by 1507 the rent had fallen to £50 owing to other mills having been established. A *doit,* meaning something small or a trifle, was originally a small copper coin from the Netherlands.

There are broadside versions under various titles (*The Contented Miller, The Jolly Miller* etc.) and an alternative set of words, from *The Universal Songster,* is printed below.

*There was a jolly miller once lived on the river Dee*
*He worked and sang from morn till night, no lark more blithe than he;*
*And this the burden of his song and ever used to be,*
*'I care for nobody, no, not I, if nobody cares for me.'*

*A noble lord, that lived hard by, sent for this miller one day,*
*And asked him various questions; and, amongst the rest did say*
*'How comes it, miller, that every day, you sing so full of glee?'*
*Quoth Ralph, 'I care for nobody if nobody cares for me.'*

*'Are you always thus contented?' To him the lord did say:*
*'Ay, that I am more happy,' quoth Ralph, 'than folks that live more gay;*
*No worldly cares disturb my breast, my wife and I agree*
*I care for nobody, no, not I, if nobody cares for me.'*

*'The reason for your happiness I would be glad to know:'*
*Quoth Ralph, 'I'll tell your lordship part of it before you go;*
*I pay my rent at quarter-day, my mind is ever free;*
*I care for nobody, no, not I, if nobody cares for me.'*

*'Thrice happy thou, who, thus content can ever merry be;*
*My whole estate I'd freely give to be as content as thee.'*
*Ralph, smiling, shook his head, and said, 'my lord that cannot be,*
*Your lordship cares for somebody, and somebody cares for thee.'*

*'How can you say so, good miller, I pray thee tell to me,*
*And, if you rightly me instruct, ten thousand shall be your fee:*
*This sum I'll give, as sure's I live, immediately unto thee,*
*When I can say, oh! Happy day, I care for nobody.'*

*Quoth Ralph, 'your lordship must refrain, where flattering knaves resort,*
*(God bless our gracious king and queen,) I mean that place, the court.*
*Leave pomp and pageantry aside, be from ambition free;*
*And then your lordship soon may sing, I care for nobody.'*

## 29. The Navigator's New Victory

Ye sportsmen of Chester I'll have ye draw near,
And of a famed runner you quickly shall hear;
I'll sing of the praise of Joe Baker by name,
And from Over, near Delamere Forest, he came.

As a navigator and runner he's known to excel,
After running, he works at the Ellesmere canal;
In going round the Roodee, which is more than a mile,
He is only five minutes and comes in with a smile.

The first was a tailor would run him, they say,
And he beat the stout tailor the whole of the way;
He led this bold hero a distance or more
And so the poor tailor was fairly done o'er.

A shoemaker next would run him, we find,
But poor Crispin was left near a distance behind;
Which grieved the runners of Chester full sore,
To find by a stranger they're fairly done o'er.

After which a chandler against him would run,
At ten in the morning, for a very large sum;
The Roodee was crowded much more that before,
But soon the fam'd chandler was fairly done o'er.

A tailor from Frodsham was grieved very much,
To hear Baker's name for running was such,
A challenge he sent him to run him once round,
In Chester race week, and the Roodee the ground.

On Thursday at ten in the morning, they met,
The course it was crowded, the weather was wet;
But the tailor and friends soon felt themselves sore,
For, ere half round, he found himself fairly done o'er.

At starting, the odds on the tailor were great,
But soon, very soon, you might see his defeat;
Ere half round, he found Baker so much far before,
He gave up the race, being so fairly done o'er.

Twenty guineas a side they run for, they say,
And many will have to long rue the day;
The navigator's friends roll in money galore
Since the Frodsham tailor he has fairly done o'er.

This broadside about a very successful long distance runner is, of course, the ballad on which Pete Coe's ever-popular song *Joseph Baker* was based. It is from the Madden Collection[3] and while no printer's name is obvious on either of the two versions available, it is likely that a Chester firm was responsible for at least one of them.

[3] A collection of over 16,000 broadsides of the late 18th and 19th century put together by Sir Frederick Madden and housed at Cambridge University Library. It is also available on microfilm at the Vaughan Williams Memorial Library, Cecil Sharp House, London.

# 30. The Norley Gate

There was a Norley fellow who owned some small estate
And sought to make it bigger with padlock fence and gate,
He knew the land was common, but didn't give a toss,
Just thought that he would try it on and fence the people's Moss.

On the tenth day of February in 1966
His minions they arrived this shameful fence to fix.
The locals grinned discretely and many the bet was cast
Just how long the time would be that ruddy fence would last.

Some told the County Council, the Parish Council too,
But soon 'twas amply evident there's nowt at all they'd do.
The Norley lads then did combine to shift that fence to hell,
But sad it is I must decline their names or rank to tell.

On a moonless night they made a start and likely lads were they;
They ripped that ruddy fence apart and bore the gate away.
Fifty quid he must have blewed to fix that fence so stout
But Norley lads, in generous mood, well they shifted it for nowt.

The police they came enquiring as to who the deed had done,
But no informer could they find, nor where that gate had gone.
Gale Moss now lies open wide with sweet gale scented still
And people there may come and bide, of its beauty drink their fill.

The sequel now I can relate, a joiner with his tools
From that oaken gate he did create some lovely little stools.
And now my story's really done, though 'tis strange I do declare
How Norley folk still sit upon a gate that isn't there.

This is the true story of what happened when one local character tried to extend his own private estate by fencing off an area that the rest of the village regarded as common land. The people of Norley objected strongly to a gated fence being erected to enclose Gale Moss and when it became clear that they were to get no support from the local authorities, took matters into their own hands. The status quo was duly restored and, as far as I am aware, the peace of the village has not been interrupted since. Reg Holmes, a resident of the area who heard the story and thought it too good a tale to pass up, wrote the song.

*Right: Reg Holmes at home in his cottage in Norley (see* The Norley Gate*). December 2004. Photo Roy Clinging*

*Left: Reg Holmes indicating the source of the spring that formed Whistlebitch Well (see song number 57). Taken in December 2004 when Reg was 91. Photo Roy Clinging*

*The gang employed to dig the saltwell at Murgatroyd's Saltworks, Brooks Lane, Middlewich, circa 1890 (see Salt Tell). My great grandfather is thought to be the third from the left in the front row.*

*Left: Jones' Ale Soulcakers at the Raven, Farndon, 1976 (see notes to The Alderley Mummers' Song and Souling Song). Saint George (Steve Tasker) looks on as The Doctor (Phil Stafford) attempts to revive Slasher (Roy Clinging) with some cavalier medical treatment. Photo Mary Clinging.*

*Above: Alderley Mummers at Alderley Park circa 1920 (see song number 2). Courtesy of Mary Houseman Private Collection. Left to Right: Enterer In: Clement Barber, Doctor: Thomas Barber, Prince Paradise: Alec Barber, St George: George Barber, Beelzebub: Ernest Barber, Colonel Slasher: Henry Barber, Young Ball (horse): Obadiah Barber, Groom: Albert Barber.*

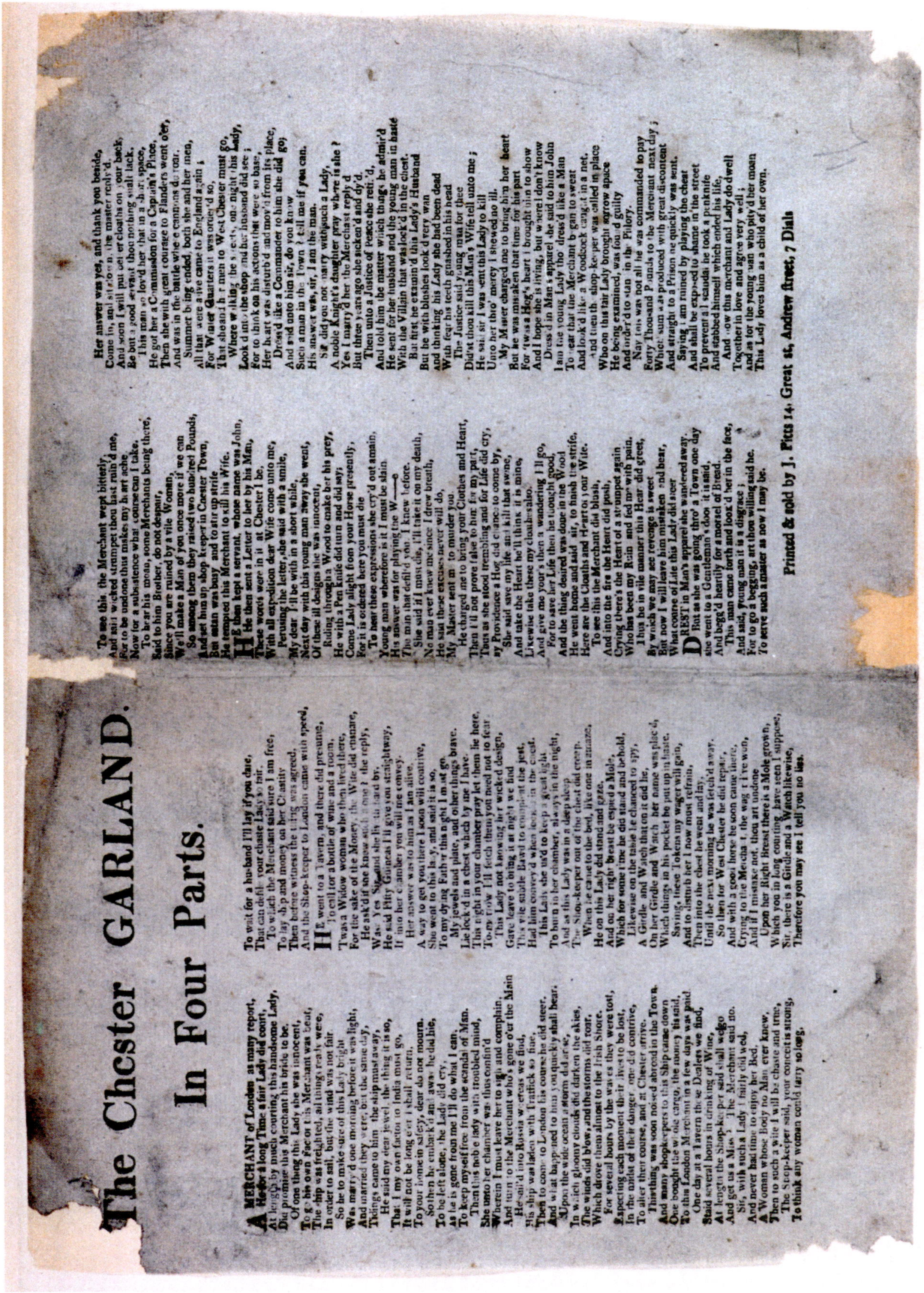

The Chester GARLAND.

In Four Parts.

Printed & sold by J. Pitts 14. Great st, Andrew street, 7 Dials

*Above: The Chester Garland (see song number 12). Printed by J Pitts of Seven Dials. From the Firth Ballads, in the Special Collections and Library Archives of Sheffield University. By permission of the Librarian, University of Sheffield Library.*

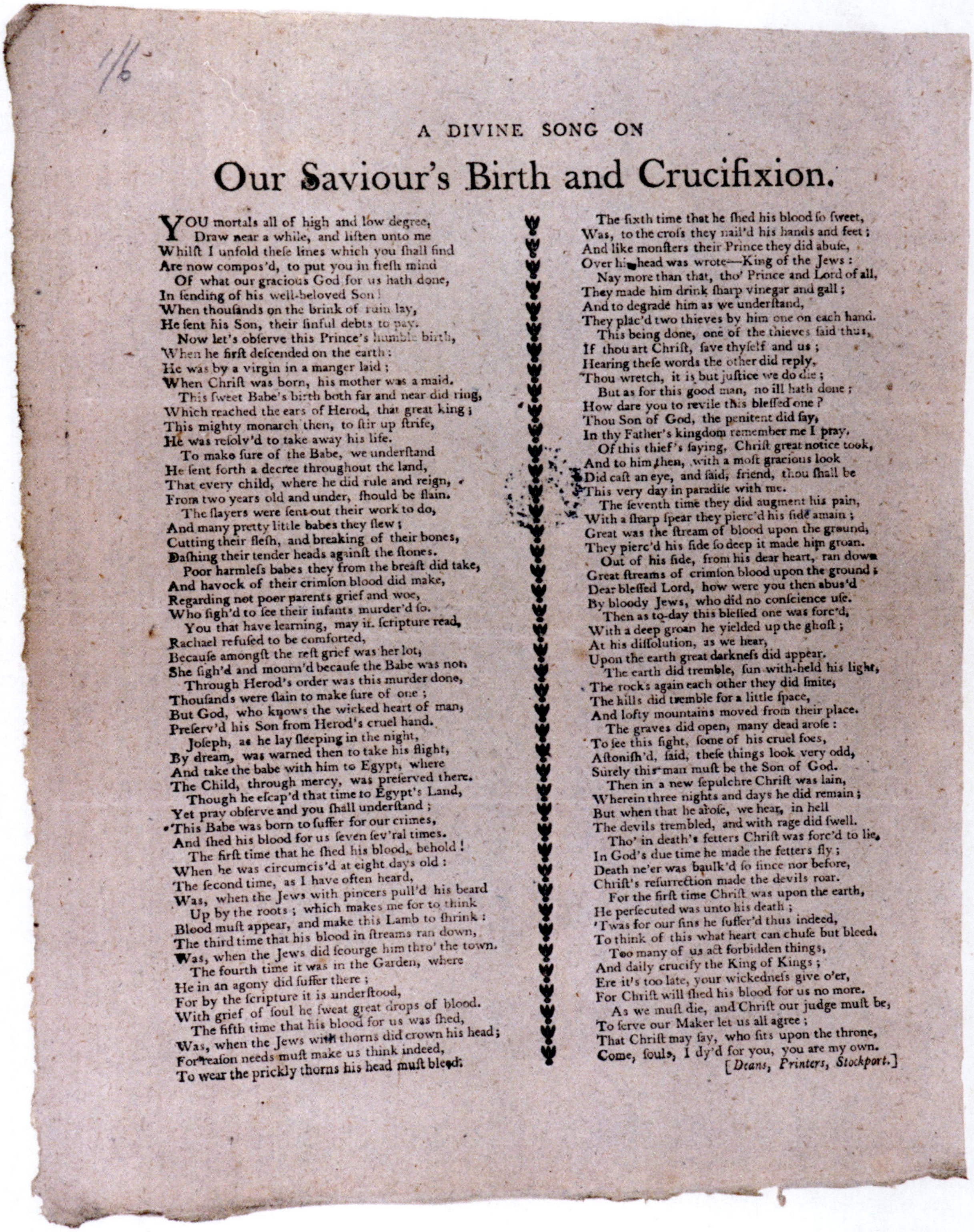

A DIVINE SONG ON

# Our Saviour's Birth and Crucifixion.

YOU mortals all of high and low degree,
Draw near a while, and liſten unto me
Whilſt I unfold theſe lines which you ſhall find
Are now compos'd, to put you in freſh mind
Of what our gracious God for us hath done,
In ſending of his well-beloved Son!
When thouſands on the brink of ruin lay,
He ſent his Son, their ſinful debts to pay.
Now let's obſerve this Prince's humble birth,
When he firſt deſcended on the earth:
He was by a virgin in a manger laid;
When Chriſt was born, his mother was a maid.
This ſweet Babe's birth both far and near did ring,
Which reached the ears of Herod, that great king;
This mighty monarch then, to ſtir up ſtrife,
He was reſolv'd to take away his life.
To make ſure of the Babe, we underſtand
He ſent forth a decree throughout the land,
That every child, where he did rule and reign,
From two years old and under, ſhould be ſlain.
The ſlayers were ſent out their work to do,
And many pretty little babes they ſlew;
Cutting their fleſh, and breaking of their bones,
Daſhing their tender heads againſt the ſtones.
Poor harmleſs babes they from the breaſt did take,
And havock of their crimſon blood did make,
Regarding not poor parents grief and woe,
Who ſigh'd to ſee their infants murder'd ſo.
You that have learning, may it. ſcripture read,
Rachael refuſed to be comforted,
Becauſe amongſt the reſt grief was her lot,
She ſigh'd and mourn'd becauſe the Babe was not.
Through Herod's order was this murder done,
Thouſands were ſlain to make ſure of one;
But God, who knows the wicked heart of man,
Preſerv'd his Son from Herod's cruel hand.
Joſeph, as he lay ſleeping in the night,
By dream, was warned then to take his flight,
And take the babe with him to Egypt, where
The Child, through mercy, was preſerved there.
Though he eſcap'd that time to Egypt's Land,
Yet pray obſerve and you ſhall underſtand;
This Babe was born to ſuffer for our crimes,
And ſhed his blood for us ſeven ſev'ral times.
The firſt time that he ſhed his blood, behold!
When he was circumcis'd at eight days old:
The ſecond time, as I have often heard,
Was, when the Jews with pincers pull'd his beard
Up by the roots; which makes me for to think
Blood muſt appear, and make this Lamb to ſhrink:
The third time that his blood in ſtreams ran down,
Was, when the Jews did ſcourge him thro' the town.
The fourth time it was in the Garden, where
He in an agony did ſuffer there;
For by the ſcripture it is underſtood,
With grief of ſoul he ſweat great drops of blood.
The fifth time that his blood for us was ſhed,
Was, when the Jews with thorns did crown his head;
For reaſon needs muſt make us think indeed,
To wear the prickly thorns his head muſt bleed.
The ſixth time that he ſhed his blood ſo ſweet,
Was, to the croſs they nail'd his hands and feet;
And like monſters their Prince they did abuſe,
Over his head was wrote—King of the Jews:
Nay more than that, tho' Prince and Lord of all,
They made him drink ſharp vinegar and gall;
And to degrade him as we underſtand,
They plac'd two thieves by him one on each hand.
This being done, one of the thieves ſaid thus,
If thou art Chriſt, ſave thyſelf and us;
Hearing theſe words the other did reply,
Thou wretch, it is but juſtice we do die;
But as for this good man, no ill hath done;
How dare you to revile this bleſſed one?
Thou Son of God, the penitent did ſay,
In thy Father's kingdom remember me I pray.
Of this thief's ſaying, Chriſt great notice took,
And to him then, with a moſt gracious look
Did caſt an eye, and ſaid, friend, thou ſhall be
This very day in paradiſe with me.
The ſeventh time they did augment his pain,
With a ſharp ſpear they pierc'd his ſide amain;
Great was the ſtream of blood upon the ground,
They pierc'd his ſide ſo deep it made him groan.
Out of his ſide, from his dear heart, ran down
Great ſtreams of crimſon blood upon the ground;
Dear bleſſed Lord, how were you then abus'd
By bloody Jews, who did no conſcience uſe.
Then as to-day this bleſſed one was forc'd,
With a deep groan he yielded up the ghoſt;
At his diſſolution, as we hear,
Upon the earth great darkneſs did appear.
The earth did tremble, ſun with-held his light,
The rocks again each other they did ſmite,
The hills did tremble for a little ſpace,
And lofty mountains moved from their place.
The graves did open, many dead aroſe:
To ſee this ſight, ſome of his cruel foes,
Aſtoniſh'd, ſaid, theſe things look very odd,
Surely this man muſt be the Son of God.
Then in a new ſepulchre Chriſt was lain,
Wherein three nights and days he did remain;
But when that he aroſe, we hear, in hell
The devils trembled, and with rage did ſwell.
Tho' in death's fetters Chriſt was forc'd to lie,
In God's due time he made the fetters fly;
Death ne'er was baulk'd ſo ſince nor before,
Chriſt's reſurrection made the devils roar.
For the firſt time Chriſt was upon the earth,
He perſecuted was unto his death;
'Twas for our ſins he ſuffer'd thus indeed,
To think of this what heart can chuſe but bleed.
Too many of us act forbidden things,
And daily crucify the King of Kings;
Ere it's too late, your wickedneſs give o'er,
For Chriſt will ſhed his blood for us no more.
As we muſt die, and Chriſt our judge muſt be,
To ſerve our Maker let us all agree;
That Chriſt may ſay, who ſits upon the throne,
Come, ſouls, I dy'd for you, you are my own.

[*Deans, Printers, Stockport.*]

*Above: Our Saviour's Birth and Crucifixion. An example of a broadside produced by Cheshire printers Deans of Stockport. From the Firth Ballads, in the Special Collections and Library Archives of Sheffield University. By permission of the Librarian, University of Sheffield Library.*

# NEW RIGS OF
# THE RACES.

TUNE—BETSY BAKER

See the ladies how they strut along,
With their sweet ruby faces,
Over nedges, ditches, gates, and stiles,
To run at ——— Races.
There's bouncing Bet, and dandy Sal,
And Eliza, blythe and bonny,
There's Tom, and Will, & swaggering Bill,
With Nancy, Dick, and Johnny.

CHORUS.

So all young men take my advice
Beware of painted faces,
And mind which way your pony runs,
When you are at the races.

See how the ladies trot along,
So charmingly and nimble,
Some think they're going to find the pea
That's underneath the thimble.
Some go for sport, some go for fun,
And some to gather riches,
And ladies go to steal the tripe
Out of the young mens breeches.

Some bet on green, and some on blue,
And some to please their fancy,
The prettiest filley on the course
Is either Peg or Nancy.
For they can either trot or run,
There must be something in it,
you can ride, just jump astride,
They'll go a mile a minute.

While the horses they are running,
Maids, and men with velvet breeches,
Will roll and tumble on the grass,
Or wallow in the ditches.
And many a maid, mark what is said
Before the race is over
Will lose her pretty m—d,
While rolling in the d ch

In nine months time some girls we'll find
To feel, I cant tell how, sir,
She will think she's in the clover field,
When milking of her cow' sir.
I am very queer, aloud she'll cry,
To work I am not able,
While John's a thrashing in the barn,
She'll be kicking in the stable.

Oh, ladies mind your P's and Q's,
This hot and searching weather,
Take my advice, dont deal too much,
In trollebobs and leather.
For if you tumble on the ground,
And roll upon your back, now,
Either Bill or Jack will soon look at
Your tit fal la ra whack, now.

All young men of each degree,
Beware and mind your riches,
Dont let the ladies steal your tripe,
Or tear your velvet breeches.
For if once they get you in a snare,
With their sweet painted faces,
You may get scorched I do declare,
Before you leave the Races.

If Johnny burns his ponys tail,
He will dance about quite nimble
And wish his peas had never been
Underneath the ladies thimble.
For cherry cheeks and ruby lips,
And charming prety faces,
Makes many a young man rue the day
He went to ——— Races.

nach, rinter, 2 , Monmouth Court, [illegible]

*Above*: *New Rigs of the Races. Printed by J Catnach of Seven Dials (see notes to* The Chester Garland*). From the Firth Ballads, in the Special Collections and Library Archives of Sheffield University. By permission of the Librarian, University of Sheffield Library.*

## BANKS OF THE DEE.

It was Summer—so softly the breezes were blowing,
And sweetly the nightingale sung from a tree,
At the foot of a rock, where the river was flowing,
I sat myself down by the side of the Dee.

Flow on, lovely Dee, flow on, thou sweet river,
Thy banks, purest stream, shall be dear to me ever
For there I first gain'd the affection and favour
Of Jemmy, the pride of the banks of the Dee.

But now he's gone from me, and left me thus mourning,
To quell the proud rebels, for valiant was he;
And yet there's no hope of his speedy returning,
To wander again on the banks of the Dee.

He's gone, hapless youth o'er the loud roaring billows,
The sweetest and kindest of all the brave fellows,
And has left me to mourn among the lov'd willows,
The loneliest maid on the banks of the Dee.

But time, and my prayers, perhaps may restore him,
Blest peace may return m
to me;
And when he comes home, with such care I'll watch over him,
He never shall quit the lov'd banks of the Dee.

The Dee still shall flow, all its beauty displaying,
The lambs and the lambkins again we shall see;
Whilst I and my Jemmy are carelessly straying,
And tasting the sweets on the banks of the Dee.

*Left: Banks of the Dee. The presence of a nightingale in this song would imply that the Dee in question is the river that flows through North Wales and Chester (rather than the Scottish river of the same name), or is this just poetic licence? Either way it is a lovely song. From the Firth Ballads, in the Special Collections and Library Archives of Sheffield University. By permission of the Librarian, University of Sheffield Library.*

## 31. The Old Man Outwitted

It's of an old farmer near Chester did dwell
Who had one daughter the truth to tell.
She was the fairest the sun shone on
But she loved his servant, a fine young man.
Early one evening the couple did meet,
Down in the shade by the garden seat.
The farmer he sat by the window above,
And he heard every word as they spoke of their love.

This caused the old farmer to fly in a rage,
And he swore that his daughter would never engage
To be married with any serving man,
So he devised a cunning plan.
And he called his servant speedily,
Said 'I must go to London would you travel with me.'
'Master, Oh master,' the young man replied,
'The thing that you ask of me won't be denied.'

Next morning for London they sped with good cheer,
And straight to the docks the old farmer did steer,
Up to a sea captain and boldly said he,
'I'm told you are looking for lads for the sea.

For I've got one here that will fit to a tee,
And thirty bright guineas I'll give to thee
If you promise you'll take him away from this shore
And swear that he'll never see home anymore.'

The captain agreed and the pressgang it went
To find this young man and on board he was sent.
But that very day I would have you to know
That the captain's lady on board did go.
She was walking the deck, her face for to fan,
And in a short while she spied the young man,
She looked in his eyes and she saw his dismay,
Saying, 'What is your trouble young sailor I pray.'

The captain then he was called over to share
The story behind this young man's despair.
When he told of the farmer and his treachery
The lady, she pleaded for his liberty.
The captain agreed and true to behold
Returned with his freedom ten guineas in gold,
Saying 'Get you to Smithfield and buy a good steed,
That will get you home first and repay this ill deed.'

He bid them adieu and to Smithfield did steer
Where he bought a good nag and did homeward repair;
And when he told his true love, she quickly agreed,
And early next morning they married with speed.
Then the young man said 'Go to my father I pray,
For I have a fancy I'd yet like to try.'
When his bride she was gone, to her chamber he goes,
And he pulls off his coat and he puts on her clothes.

Then he sat himself down by the fire to spin,
And just as he started the old man came in
Crying 'Daughter, dear daughter I would have you take care,
For I've broke the intrigues between you and your dear.
For he's gone from this shore where the wild billows roar
And he never will see dear old England no more.'
The young man turned round, 'Cruel master,' cried he,
'You have sent your own daughter away to the sea.'

'For she heard that to London I must go with you
And she had such desires that city to view
That she begged and she craved, till I did agree
She could dress in my clothes and pretend to be me.'
Then the old man he turned and away he did run
He was tearing his hair crying, 'What have I done.'
He ran to the barn, for a beam he did make
With a rope round his neck, his life for to take.

But the young man was quick, and he soon cut him free
Saying 'I'll do my best to return her to thee.'
'Then five hundred pounds to you I shall give,
And the hand of my daughter if she still do live.'
But now the young man weren't so willing to trust

And made sure that the bargain was written down first;
And when it was signed to his bride he did run
And he told her the story of what he had done.

Then early next morning the young man arose
And along with his bride to the farmer he goes.
And now the young couple the truth did reveal,
And craving his blessing, before him did kneel.
'I'll give you my blessing,' was the old man's reply,
'And ten thousand pounds you shall have when I die.
For I thought my daughter was taken from me,
But now I'm well paid for my own trickery.'

The story of the young girl falling in love with a servant only to earn the wrath of her disapproving father is a common one in traditional song. The actions of the angry father vary from song to song and in *Her Servant Man*, a version collected by Bob Copper of the famous Sussex singing family, the poor girl is locked in an underground dungeon, fed only on bread and water, and soundly beaten three times a day – for her own good, of course. Whatever trials they have to endure, however, the love of the young couple usually prevails, although the extra twist of the young man turning the tables and outwitting the old farmer is new to me. The original text is from Egerton Leigh's *Ballads and Legends of Cheshire* but was reproduced from an earlier volume, Halliwell's *Palatine Anthology*, where it was supposed by Mr Halliwell to date from around the middle of the eighteenth century.

Not all such tales of love across the social divide have a happy ending though, as the following verse from *The Universal Songster* (Vol 1, p23) shows. In *Cheshire Gleanings* William Axon refers to the same song calling it simply *Cheshire Ballad*.

*In Chester town there lived a lad,*
*As many lads there be;*
*He was a buxom boy, adad,*
*And loved a fair lady.*

*He was a serving man by trade,*
*But luckless was his doom;*
*He loved the mistress, not the maid,*
*Which brought him to his tomb.*

*You might have heard this lover's groans,*
*Full sorely did he smart;*
*Her cruel hands they broke his bones,*
*Her cruel eyes his heart.*

## 32. Old Reynard's Got Away

O'er hill and dale the echoes sail, 'tis the merry huntsman's horn
Across Hatchmere, the note rings clear on a pleasant autumn morn.
The hounds are baying, the horn is saying 'Come hunt with us today!'
In the forest green, Tawny Red is seen, bold Reynard's on his way.

Chorus: *View Hallo–a! Doory doory doory Ha ha ha!*
*Tally ho! Old Reynard's got away.*

Across Red Hollow the hounds they follow old Reynard in his flight.
He crossed the road and never slowed to scale the old Pale Height.
Through bush and break, around Black Lake, he found no place to hide,
With panting breath and fearing death he jumped the Battleaxe Ride.

By Hornsby's Rough, in Gallows Clough, the old fox doubled back,
He breasted the ridge by the station bridge, so dodged the yelping pack.
Through the station yard, they pressed him hard, he escaped along the rail,
So past the box they chased the fox just a-hint his brushy tail.

'Tis my belief that sly old thief, he knew his train times well,
For the Chester train on the upside main scattered those hounds to hell.
The huntsmen cried, they damn near died, as the train went thundering by
And up the batter they were forced to scatter to watch three young hounds die.

When the whistle blew the old fox knew he'd escaped those hounds and men,
Leaving three hounds dead away he fled to his earthy forest den.
Through the forest rides there still he glides, by night he raids for fowl,
On a frosty night in the pale moonlight, well you'll know him by his howl.

Written by Reg Holmes, an ex-railwayman, this is a hunting song where the fox wins. He recalls that in 1972 while working in the signal box on the Delamere to Mouldsworth line he heard the sound of a hunting horn nearby. He looked round and was surprised to see the fox, closely followed by the hunt, coming along the railway line. With a train fast approaching drastic action had to be taken and the hunt scrambled up the side of the embankment and escaped by means of an iron railing that could be lifted out of its mountings (this was only possible if enough people were present to do it). The hunt escaped with the loss of only three hounds, considerably less than it could have been, and the driver of the train was clearly shaken by the experience and stopped at the signal box to gather his wits. He complained loudly that situations like this should not be allowed to happen and Reg, of course, informed him that he could not be held responsible as the hounds had completely ignored his signal. The song includes many place names that will be familiar to regular visitors to the Delamere Forest area. *The rides* are passes through the forest, *the batter* is the slope from the railway line to the fence at the top of a cutting, and *a-hint* means behind.

## 33. Pace Egging Song

Here comes three or four jovie lads, all of one mind,
We've come a pace eggin', we hope you'll prove kind,
Prove kind, prove kind, with your eggs and small beer,
We hope you'll remember it's pace eggin' time

Chorus: *For the diddle dol, for the day, for the diddle dol de day*

The next that comes in is Lord Nelson, you see,
With a bunch of blue ribbon tied under the knee;
With a star on his breast, like a diamond do shine,
I hope you'll remember it's pace eggin' time.

The next that comes in is the miner, you see,
With his round hat and candle he works underground;
He works underground to get neighbour's coal,
At six in the morning he pops down yond hole.

Pace Egging was an Easter celebration widely practised in the north western counties of Cheshire, Lancashire, Westmorland, Cumberland and parts of Yorkshire. This version is from Marple where Mr Arthur Hulme remembered it being sung between 1895 and 1900. Other instances are recorded in Neston, Staleybridge, and Stockport and in 1907 Samuel Hill, recalling his memories of his life in Staleybridge, mentioned a past performer of what he referred to as 'peace' egging as saying:

*'We were always sure of getting something at the house of Mr and Mrs Platt, not from Mr Platt, but from his lady. Sometimes there would be twelve or fourteen of us, and a rough lot we were. Ranged against the wall of the yard near the house, we went through our play-acting, and on its conclusion we each got a gill pot full of milk and a new laid egg, together with a threepenny bit. Ah! Masters were masters in those days.'*

On the Wirral children would go round chanting hoping to receive a reward of eggs, usually boiled very hard and sometimes coloured by an infusion of herbs.

*Please, Mr Whiteley,*
*Please give us an Easter egg.*
*If you do not give us one*
*Your hen shall lay an addled one,*
*Your cock shall lay a stone.*

Hilda Gamlin in *Memories of Birkenhead* (1892) recalls that on Easter Monday the children would bring baskets of coloured eggs to the park and the best assortment would win a prize before using them for a game. This involved the erection of a series of 'wickets' at the foot of a hill, then the children took their eggs to the top and rolled them down, hoping to pass them, unbroken, between the wickets. Again prizes were given to the best performers. She goes on:

*'A large crowd of people always assembled to witness these sports, which included the "Easter Egg Dance," executed by the young people, who were then regaled on buns.'*

In 1884 William Axon wrote:

*'The name of 'pace-egg' is also given to a species of rustic drama, once an invaluable accompaniment to this season, and very popular in all parts of Cheshire and the adjoining counties. The construction was one that readily admitted of the interpolation of any new character that happened to come before the public. Thus, the spectators were treated to the somewhat anomalous appearance of Lord Nelson, the Duke of Wellington, or any other popular hero, along with St George of England and his redoubtable antagonist The Soldan of Babylon. Sometimes girls were dressed up to enact the male parts, whilst usually the 'Bessy' – a very low comedy character – was undertaken by a youth. The 'Fool', in addition to his other vocation, acted as a sort of master of ceremonies, and in that capacity announced St George in a lofty strain of appreciative names – some marking his valourous deeds – after which 'enter Slasher', who is even more boastful than the patron saint, and, the two having fought, Slasher is wounded, but recovers by the care of a miraculous doctor. St George next fights with the Black Prince of Paradine, whom he slays, and then the King of Egypt, the father of the dead Prince, brings forward Hector, who is also wounded. The fool next challenged the Saint, and an appointment is made for a combat. They leave, and then the finale appears in the person of a diabolical personage, who firmly but respectfully remarks:*

*Here come I, little Devil Doubt;*
*If you do not give me money,*
*I'll sweep you all out.*
*Money I want, and money I crave:*
*If you do not give me money,*
*I'll sweep you to the grave.*

*The appeal for money was not made in vain, as the sweeping out demonstration was far too realistic to be pleasant. The libretto of the astounding drama of the "pace-egg" appears to be some two centuries old.'*

# 34. The 'Prentice Boy

I'm a 'prentice boy, my name is Bob,
The tale I've oft related,
They bound me to a dirty snob,
A trade I always hated.
The lapstone I did daily shun,
The sight of a stirrup alarmed me;
So off I run with my master's gun
To enlist in the Spanish army.

Chorus: *With my master's gun, my master's gun, I fought my way to glory.*

Some balls of wax with hemp and tacks
I thought might be required
To give our foes some precious whacks
When all the shots were fired.
In battle I did mock their tricks,
And when they thought of beating,
I fired my wax against their backs
And sent them all retreating.

Then I took out my hemp so fine
That was in my knapsack hoarded,
Among their troops I did entwine,
Which now you find recorded.
At legs and arms I fire away,
And some of their knobs I twisted;
Thinks I, I'll make them rue the day
That a 'prentice boy enlisted.

And soon I brought their colour down,
Which caused a great attraction,
And did my head with honour crown,
What glorious satisfaction!
General Evans comes up to me,
Says he, 'Bob, show no quarter,
You're a valiant youth, I plainly see,
And you shall marry my daughter.'

You'll hear of my fame where'er you walk,
In songs and magazines too,
And shall for ever be the talk
Of soldiers and marines, too.
I will say before I make my bow,
Though perhaps you may laugh hearty,
I'm called by all the Spaniards now
'The British Buonaparté.'

The text of this song was collected by H E D Hammond from Lt Col W Gostwyck-Gostwyck from Chester. The tune and chorus, however, have been added from a similar version noted from Mr Henry Athrelpo of Bath in 1907. A *snob* was a colloquial term for a cobbler or shoemaker and *knob* (or *nob*) is slang for head.

# 35. The Rambling Royal

Oh, I am a rambling Royal, from Liverpool I came,
And to my sad misfortune I enlisted in the Marines.
Being drunk when I enlisted, not knowing what I'd done,
Until my sober senses returned to me again.

Well, I had a girl in Birkenhead, a true friend, as it seems.
It broke her heart and made her smart to see me in the Marines;
She said, 'If you desert, young man, as I do hope you may,
I'll have you in my own bedroom if you should chance to stay.'

It was at the Chatham Depot the officer gave command
That me and two of my comrades that night on guard should stand.
The night being dark and wet and cold, with me did not agree,
So I knocked out a guardroom corporal and ran for my liberty.

Oh, I rambled all that livelong night until I lost my way,
And I landed in some farmer's barn and stretched out on the hay.
When I awoke it was no joke for there all at my head
The sergeant and the officer and two bloody swaddies stood.

Well, we had a terrible fight and I damn near beat them all;
I made my cowardly comrades in agony to bawl,
But they locked me in the glasshouse my sorrows to deplore,
With a man at every window and a man at every door.

It was early the very next morning, I paced the guardhouse round;
I jumped out of a window and felled three of them to the ground,
But the provost and his bullies, they was quickly after me,

But I made my way to Birkenhead and so gained my liberty.

Oh, I am a rambling Royal, James Cronin is my name;
I can fight as many officers as you'll find in the Marines.
I can fight as many Orangemen as ever banged a drum,
And I'll make 'em run before me like a bullet from a gun.

Songs dealing with great exploits and heroism in battle are common, but the subject here is the resolve and determination required to run away from the military. A young man joins the Royal Marines while under the influence of alcohol and then continually tries to desert, eventually succeeding with the help of his girlfriend in Birkenhead. The *glasshouse* is a guardroom or military prison, and the *provost* would be the sergeant in charge of the military police.

The song is probably based on an Irish rebel ballad of the late 18th century called *The Bold Belfast Shoemaker* the last verse of which runs:

*I am a bold shoemaker and Irewin is my name*
*I could beat as many Orangemen as listed on a train;*
*I could beat as many Orangemen as could stand in a row*
*I would make them fly before me like an arrow from a bow.*

## 36. Remember

Is that the sword that I used in the war?
What is that word engraved on it for?
That blade, nephew mine, for the Martyr-King fought;
And that was the message that Gabriel brought
When he rode to tell of the murder they wrought.
'Twas the Kings last word to his own true men;
And you hear it now as I heard it then,
In the roar of the wind and the Causeway.

'Twas a night like this, for the moon was high,
With drifting clouds in the moonlit sky.
I was dozing alone in the ingle-seat,
When the clatter of hooves rang out in the street,
Then the shouting of men and the tramping of feet.
I hasted to ask 'What news do you bring?'
And the horseman said 'They have slain the King!'
In the roar of the wind and the Causeway.

He went to his death with a martyr's tread.
A single word to the Bishop he said:
And bade him 'Remember!' 'twas meant for us all;
And, comrades, we will, by the crime of Whitehall;
The vengeance of God on the regicides fall!
And still in my ears rings the bitter wail
That mingled that night in the winter's gale,
And the roar of the wind and the Causeway.

We thought of the day when the King had seen
The rebels defeat us on Rowton Green.
From the North-East tower he had followed the fight,
And we thought of his ride to the West that night,
And how the old city had fought for the right.
And our hearts were bitter, for hope had fled,
And we heard that night that the King was dead,
In the roar of the wind and the Causeway.

So the King's last word I cut on my sword,
And deep on my heart his message is scored!
But Merrie Old England is merry again,
For a Stuart once more a monarch doth reign!
On that May-Day in Chester this was the strain —
'God save Lord Byron and God save the King!'
And loud the old walls of the city did ring,
To the roar of the guns and the Causeway.

This gem, from *Cheshire Notes and Queries,* was found in a section entitled *'Poets Corner'* which appears to have been for local contributions. It was captioned *'T.T.H. in the Chester Courant'*. The *'Chester Courant'* was a weekly newspaper specialising in local affairs, and this was no doubt reproduced from an earlier edition. The identity of T.T.H., however, remains a mystery, as does the caption under the title which reads *'Told by a gentleman of Bridge Place, Chester, to his nephew in 1665'*. How nice it would be if this were true, but I have so far been unable to either prove or disprove the statement.

I had wanted to sing this as a song for some time, but could not find, or make up, a tune to fit and so I eventually asked my good friend Mal Waite if she could help. She took the words away and came back with this beautiful tune in a ridiculously short space of time. Aren't some people annoying?

*Lord Byron* is a reference to Chester's military governor. The first military governor of Chester was Sir Nicholas Byron and, after his capture at Ellesmere in January 1644, his nephew John, Lord Byron, commander of the royalist forces in Cheshire was chosen to replace him.

# 37. The Rich Farmer in Cheshire

It's of a rich farmer in Cheshire,
To market his daughter did go,
And thinking that no one would harm her
As she'd oft-times been that road before.
And thinking that no one would harm her
As she'd oft-times been that road before.

But she met with a lusty highwayman
A pistol he held at her breast,
'Deliver your money, your clothing,
Or else you will die in distress.'
'Deliver your money, your clothing,
Or else you will die in distress.'

He hipped her and stripped her stark naked,
And gave her the bridle to hold,
There she stood shivering and shaking,
Almost starving to death with the cold.
There she stood shivering and shaking,
Almost starving to death with the cold.

But being a buxom young damsel,
She faced him as though unafraid,
One slash from her whip sent him sprawling
His pistols she took as he lay.
One slash from her whip sent him sprawling
His pistols she took as he lay.

She put her left foot in the stirrup
And mounted his horse like a man,
Over hedges and ditches she galloped
'Oh catch me you old rogue if you can.'
Over hedges and ditches she galloped
'Oh catch me you old rogue if you can.'

'Oh, daughter, oh, daughter, what kept you,
What kept you at market so long?'
'Oh father, I fell in great danger,
But the rogue he has done me no wrong.'
'Oh father, I fell in great danger,
But the rogue he has done me no wrong.'

They led the grey mare to the stable,
And laid a white cloth on the floor,
And there she sat counting the money
And she's counted five thousand in gold!
And there she sat counting the money
And she's counted five thousand in gold!

A countrywide favourite among traditional singers, I first learned this from the singing of Mal Waite and have combined it with another set of words found in *Ballads and Legends of Cheshire*. Although a variant of the song was sometimes sung at the end of a performance by the Soulers of Lower Withington and Lower Peover, this longer ballad version is much more widespread.

## 38. Rope Dance

They call me John Lomas from Audlem I came;
Don't take my slippery slope.
Good people attend to these words I have penned,
For I'll dance at the end of a rope, a rope,
For I'll dance at the end of a rope.

Now I had a good master and worked very hard,
But the mistress on me cast an eye;
Said if I set her free, her lover I'd be,
But her husband would first have to die, to die,
But her husband would first have to die.

So I did consent to do this foul deed
And with liquor her good man was plied,
And then as we planned, with an axe in my hand
I struck him and hoped he had died, had died,
I struck him and hoped he had died.

But he rose in his gore, so we struck him again
With a razor which by the bed lay;
But the blood that he spilt on my shirt proved my guilt,
And in irons they took me away, away,
And in irons they took me away.

Her husband was dead and her lover was taken.
That very same razor she found,
And that murdering wife, she took her own life,
And they buried them in the same ground, same ground,
And they buried them in the same ground.

They call me John Lomas, from Audlem I came;
Don't take my slippery slope.
Farewell Chester gaol, I have told my sad tale,

Now I'll dance at the end of a rope, a rope,
Now I'll dance at the end of a rope.

This is another version of the story of John Lomas and his part in the Hankelow murders [see *John Lomas's Farewell*], again in broadside style, and written by Peter Massey and Gordon Morris.

# 39. Salt Tell

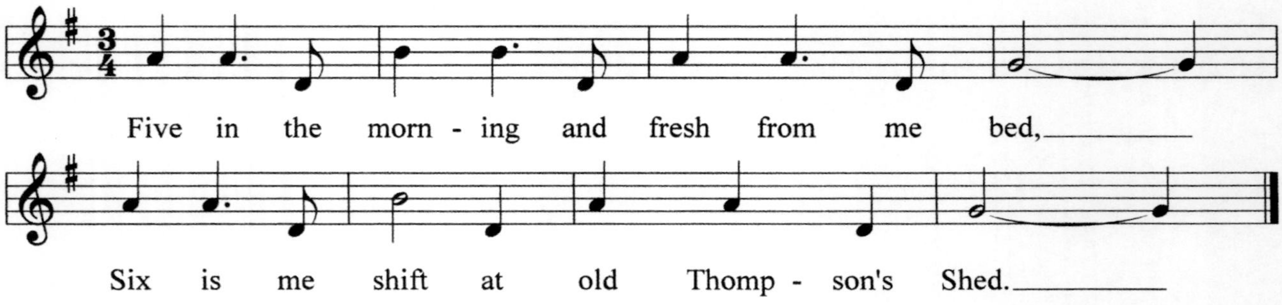


Five in the morning and fresh from me bed,
Six is me shift at old Thompson's Shed.
The flashes are frozen, the road's getting hard,
Over the lime-beds to the salt house yard.
Marston looks miserable, Wincham is wet,
But the foreman will soon have me working a sweat
The wheel on the pump house goes round and round,
Wild brine comes rushing up out of the ground.

Down through the pipes to the red iron pan,
Bass the fire Johnny as quick as you can.
Rake out the clinker, give the fire a blast,
Stoke on the coal so the brine boils up fast.
The heat's like a jungle, the steam's like a fog,
And I'm stripped to the waist in me flannel and clogs.
The wheel on the pump house goes round and round,
Wild brine comes rushing up out of the ground.

The water's boiled off and the salt's left behind,
Old Charlie comes in, the best waller you'll find.
The salt's on his tongue and his mind's on the pub,
As he skims the wet salt from the pan to the tubs.
Load up the barrow and cart them away,
They'll dry in the flue room by the end of the day.
The wheel on the pump house goes round and round,
Wild brine comes rushing up out of the ground.

Lumps of white marble standing in line,
Or piled up in sacks, if the salt's good and fine.
Fill up the barges, load after load;
Salt for the table, salt for the road,
Salt for the farmer, for factory and town.
The wheel on the pump house goes round and round.
The wheel on the pump house goes round and round,
Wild brine comes rushing up out of the ground.

Much salt production came from a technique known as 'wild brine pumping' which involved sending hot water underground, thus dissolving the salt, and then pumping the brine back to the surface and into large vats, known as pans, which were kept at a high enough temperature for the water to evaporate so that the salt residue could be taken off the surface and put into tubs. This was naturally very hot, humid and thirsty work, which probably explains why there always seemed an abundance of public houses in the salt towns. The men had flannel tunics, though photographs show they often worked stripped to the waist, flannel trousers and wooden soled clogs and would wear extra protection on their lower legs and feet in case of splashing, as the brine was hot enough to scald. In the nineteenth century it was common for women to work alongside the men and because of the heat they stripped to their undergarments. This came to be considered indecent and in the 1870s led to unfounded attacks on their morals and reports that they were in the habit of working almost naked. To add insult to injury the work was accompanied by the incessant repetitive monotonous rhythm of the wheel pumping the brine up the shaft and into the pans, cleverly represented in this song (written by Pete & Chris Coe) by the constantly repeating tune. Pete's father worked at the Lion Salt Works in Wincham (before moving to ICI) and so gave him detailed information on the workings of the salt industry.

The three main salt producing towns of Middlewich, Nantwich and Northwich – often referred to as the *Cheshire Wiches* – assumed great importance as suppliers of this vital commodity which was a major source of income and essential for the seasoning and preservation of meat and fish. Due largely to their economic importance, the Domesday Book deals with the *Wiches* in a section to themselves, and there is evidence that salt pits were worked here as long ago as Roman times, when present-day Middlewich was known as *Salinae*.

In *Ballads and Legends of Cheshire* (Egerton Leigh 1867) he says:

*'On Ascension day, in days long past, the inhabitants of Nantwich used to assemble in gala dress round the 'Old Biat' salt pit, which was ornamented for the occasion with flowers and all procurable rustic finery, and pass the day in dancing, feasting, and merriment. This was called Blessing the Brine.'*

*Wreaths of varied hues we bring,*
*Flowers of the early spring,*
*Hand in hand we join a ring,*
*Round Old Biat pit to sing,*
*God bless the Brine.*

The extraction of such large amounts of salt created a massive subsidence problem, however, and I was often told that the people of Northwich had to go up a step into their houses at night, and up a step to come out again in the morning. My mother recalls a Salt Works building along the Trent and Mersey canal in Middlewich which was affected so much by subsidence that it became unusable overnight, eventually sinking altogether, and my brother and I would go fishing for sticklebacks in the pools that are all that now remain on the site. She also remembers an old Flint Mill, along the same stretch of canal, which was there one day, and completely gone the next. Needless to say local solicitors are still obliged to conduct a brine search whenever a property changes hands in the area, as subsidence is still a major concern.

# 40. Sands of Dee

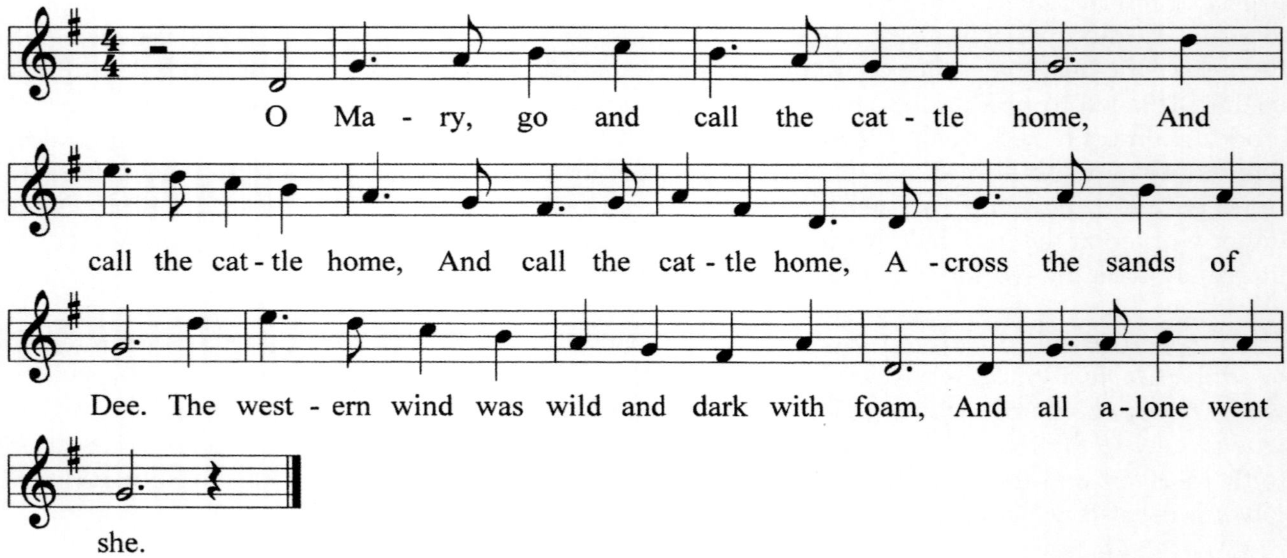


O Mary, go and call the cattle home,
And call the cattle home,
And call the cattle home,
Across the sands of Dee.
The western wind was wild and dark with foam,
And all alone went she.

The western tide crept up along the sand,
And o'er and o'er the sand,
And round and round the sand,
As far as the eye could see.
The rolling mist swept down, and hid the land,
And never home came she!

O is it weed, or fish, or floating hair?
A tress of golden hair,
A drowned maidens hair,
Above the nets at sea;
Was never salmon yet that shone so fair
Among the stakes at Dee.

They rowed her in across the rolling foam,
The cruel crawling foam,
The cruel hungry foam,
To her grave beside the sea!
But still the boatmen hear her call her cattle home
Across the sands of Dee.

When the tide is out the Dee estuary exposes a vast expanse of sand and the islands of Hilbre, Middle Eye, and Little Eye can easily be reached on foot, but in poor visibility, with no landmarks to speak of, it can be a completely different story. The words, a poem by Charles Kingsley (1819-1875), first appeared in 1850 in his novel *Alton Locke* about a young tailor who used poetry as a voice against social injustice. It has been the subject of numerous musical settings; most people I know who sing the song use a different melody, and this one is my own.

The basis for the story is unknown but on a visit to Hoylake in 2001 I met Mrs Lee Ireland who told me the tale as she knew it. Mrs Ireland informed me that local legend has it that the song was based on her husband's great, great grandmother who lived on Hilbre and would bring her sheep across the estuary to market in West Kirby. She had long flowing red hair which would stream out behind her as she rode on her chestnut gelding and by the time she reached West Kirby it was impossible to tell which was her hair and which was the horse's tail as the two mingled together in the wind. This became something of a regular occurrence until the day of her disappearance. She set off for the mainland in her usual way, but when her horse arrived in West Kirby, she was nowhere to be seen.

# 41. The Shocklach Carol

Come all ye true good Christians that liveth here on earth
Let us celebrate this morning of our sweet Saviour's birth
This is the happy hour this is the blessed morn
For to save our souls from sin this Lamb of God was born

It was the angel Gabriel in scripture it was read
Went with that holy message unto a virgin maid
'Hail blessed amongst all women' he kindly said 'Oh then
Thou shalt be the mother to the saviour of all men'

Then this replied the virgin 'How must I bear or can
For to receive a saviour when I never knew a man'
And this replied the Angel 'These things shall surely be
For the power of the Almighty shall over shadow thee

Rejoice at these glad tidings which cometh from the Lord
And be thou forth his handmaiden according to his word'
And this replied the virgin 'These things I know right well
There has been no such wonder no not in Israel'

Her time it being accomplished to Bethlehem she come
And here this blessed virgin was delivered of a son
No princely pomp attended His honour was but small
For a manger was His cradle His bed an oxen stall

At twelve years old they found Him all in the temple sat
Amongst those learned doctors which were renowned for wit

Hearing and answering questions at which they wondered all
Because they knew for certain that His learning was but small

Then He did many wonders Oh then from time to time
He turned the clearest water into the purest wine
He cleansed the bloody issue the lame He made to walk
The blind their sight receiveth likewise the dumb to talk

And He did many wonders Oh then from day to day
Until that wretched Judias [sic] he did our Lord betray
Into the hands of sinners those violent bloody Jews
And they with many a torment did basely Him abuse

They led Him unto Pilot who Governor was then
For to receive His sentence as the vilest of all men
His innocence foresended they would Him crucify
And by the hands of sinners this Lamb of God must die

When he on the cross was suffering He to his father called
'They know not what they are doing I pray forgive them all'
For the space of three long hours there was darkness over the earth
And all the whole creation did tremble at His death

The rocks did burst asunder the temple rent in twain
And all the graves flew open when the Lamb of God was slain
All things were full of terror of this most shocking sight
Then said the great Centurion this is the God of might

Then Joseph went to Pilot and did His body crave
For to have it rightly buried all in a new made grave
The third day in the morning He arose up from the dead
And by God's holy angels to heaven He was led

The third day in the morning unto the grave they went
To anoint His holy body it was their full intent
Appeared to them an angel which said 'The truth will tell
That Christ Himself has risen He has conquered death and hell'

To Him who has ascended let all our praises be
And we His steps might follow and Him our pattern be
For when our days are ended we soon shall hear Him call
'Come ye blessed of my kingdom it's prepared for you all!'

It would seem that carol singing was a popular activity in this part (the south) of the county. This carol was performed around the village of Shocklach on Christmas Eve (often between 10pm and 4am) and nearby Malpas is reputed to have had its own version which stretched to a mighty 42 verses. It was collected in December 1957 by Brian Ballinger who got the words from Mr Tom Clarke who used to play the melodeon and harmonica for the carol up to the early 1950s when they stopped singing it round the village. The tune is from Mr J S Sudlow, who also used to sing the carol which he learnt from his father.

A similar song, under the title of *The Angel Gabriel*, has been recorded from oral tradition in other parts of the country (though, sadly, not Cheshire) and has also appeared in broadside form from the late 17th century onwards.

# 42. Souling Song

We are one, two, three hearty lads, and we're all of one mind
We have come a-souling good nature to find
We've all come a-souling as it doth appear
And all that we are souling for is your ale and strong beer

Turn out all you young men and you maidens also
And if you are willing with us you shall go
We will bring you safe back you've no need to fear
And all that we're a-souling for is your ale and strong beer

Dear mistress, dear mistress do not tarry to spin
But look for a jug for to put some ale in
And when we have got it how soon you shall see
That when we have drunk it how merry we'll be

Go down to your cellar and there you will find
Good ale, beer and brandy and the best of old wine
And if you will bring us a jug of your beer
We'll not come a-souling till this time next year

God bless the master and the mistress also
And all the young children that round the house go
Your men and maidens your cattle and store
And all that is in your gates we wish you ten times more

Many songs have been collected in connection with the tradition of soul-caking, or souling, with practically every village having its own version. This one was sent to the Journal of the English Folk Dance & Song Society in 1938 by a Miss Witham from Chester.

Traditional dramas (sometimes referred to by the all-encompassing title of mumming plays) have been collected from all corners of the country. They are usually associated with one particular season and as such are commonly referred to as 'calendar customs' – that is to say that within any one community the play is always performed at the same time of year. There are significant variations on this but in Cheshire plays were performed on three main occasions – at the end of October / early November (souling), Christmas (mumming), and Easter (pace egging) – which basically covered the old style winter months. All of the plays seem to be of the 'hero-combat' or 'death and resurrection' style i.e. the hero (usually a variation of Saint George) fights with one or two adversaries, one of whom is killed and brought back to life again. While the basic plot is always the same there is a huge array of local variations and characters. *St George* is sometimes *King George*; the first actor who sets the scene may be the *Enterer In*, the *Letter In*, or the *Door Opener*; some plays have an old woman who mourns the passing of the slain knight; some have a character call *Little Devil* (or *Derry* or *Jerry* or *Dicky*) *Dout*[4] whose contribution to the plot is usually minimal; there is always a horse who may be called *Dick*, *Young Ball*, or simply the *Wild Horse*. The list goes on and on. The actors were always well received, as the plays were thought to bring good luck, and they were often given refreshment or supplied with apples, drink and small, sweet, lightly spiced cakes, called soul-cakes.

[4] According to Thomas Darlington (*The Folk Speech of South Cheshire*, 1887) *Dicky Dout* was a person whose shirt was visible below the waistcoat and the following rhyme would be used:

'Dicky, Dicky Dout, Yur Shirt Hangs out, Four yards in, an' five yards out.'

# 43. Souling Song – Guilden Sutton

We are one, two, three hearty lads, we are all of one mind,
We have come a-souling this night to make clear
That if you will draw us a mug of good beer,
We won't come no more a-souling until another year.
Fol the diddle dol, fol the day, fol the diddle dol di day.

The first verse is sung outside the door before the action begins. After the play is completed the actors are introduced in song, each walking round the room as his character is mentioned.

The first that steps in is a soldier you see
He has been a-fighting thro' the ocean all round
He has fought thro' France and likewise thro' Spain
And now he has returned to old England again
Fol the diddle dol, fol the day, fol the diddle dol di day.

The next that steps in is a sailor you see,
He has been a-fighting thro' the ocean all round;
He has fought thro' France and likewise thro' Spain
And now he has returned to old England a-gain
Fol the diddle dol, fol the day, fol the diddle dol di day.

And the next that steps in is a lady you see,
With her hat, cap, and feather she looks very gay.
With her hat, cap, and feather she looks very fine,
And all that she delights in is drinking red wine,
Fol the diddle etc.

And the next that steps in is a doctor you see,
He has been a-quacking thro' the ocean all round.
He been a-quacking thro' France and likewise thro' Spain
And now he has returned to old England a-gain,
Fol the diddle etc.

And the next that steps in is a miser you see,
He ate all his money and he wears his old rags.
And he wears them so near, and he sells them so dear
That no-one will buy them until another year
Fol the diddle etc.

And now to conclude and to finish we must,
Put your hand in your pocket and pull out your purse.
Put your hand in your pocket and see if it's all right,
If you give us nowt, we'll take nowt, farewell and goodnight!
Fol the diddle etc.

From the *Journal of the English Folk Dance and Song Society*, December 1947, this intriguing version was communicated by Catherine Cathcart-Smith. The ending, introducing all the characters in song, makes an interesting variation on the more usual theme of all the actors being in the room at the end of the play and singing together. The first verse – *The first that steps in is a soldier you see* – gives *King George* his opportunity to present himself to the audience. The *sailor* verse represents the *Turkish Knight* and the three remaining verses (the *lady*, the *doctor*, and the *miser*) are the chance for *Martha*, the *Doctor* and *Paddywhack* to show off. The final verse is sung all together.

# 44. Souling Song – Stapleford

We are one, two, three, good hearty lads, we are all in one mind,
We have all come a-souling, good nature to find.
And if you will give us one jug of your beer,
We will not come a-souling till this time next year.

Step down in your cellar and see what you'll find,
There is ale, rum, gin and brandy, and all kind of wine.
And if you will give us one jug of beer,
We'll not come a-souling till this time next year.

God bless the master of this house and the mistress also,
And all the little children round the table do go;
Likewise your men and maidens, your cattle and store,
And it's all that lies within you, we will wish you ten times more.

Collected by Duncan Broomhead from Mr James Henry (Harry) Lee of Kelsall, who also supplied a full text of the play and descriptions of costume detail. Harry recalled starting Souling when he was twelve until the outbreak of the First World War. He learnt the play from his parents, family and neighbours and performed it around the farms, cottages, large houses and pubs over a wide area including Stapleford, Hargrave, Duddon, Barrow and Tarporley.

Each year the gang, all local youths, would build themselves a rough wooden hut out of sticks and planks and practise for a couple of weeks before they went out. They took a collection after each performance, which was mostly spent on fireworks, and also received gifts of homemade cake and free beer at the pubs. He also mentioned going to Stapleford Hall each year knowing that they would be given half a crown just to go away.

While there are written texts of many of these plays currently available in libraries and archives, performers like Harry would have learned their parts by the oral tradition – that is to say that it is not written down but passed on by word of mouth from one generation to the next. This method of learning a part can lead to words gradually changing over the years as different people portray their role in a slightly different manner, or sometimes things are simply misheard or a word is used that the listener is unfamiliar with and so he replaces it with something that sounds similar to the original and makes more sense to him. For example the character of Beelzebub, the devil, is sometimes known as *Belzebub*, or even *Bellsie Bob*[5], and when he enters in some versions he announces that *'over my shoulder I carry a club,'* while in others he carries *'a clog'* and occasionally *'a clod'*. Such variations are legion.

[5] My favourite of these variations comes from the Midlands. In the *Evesham Journal* of Saturday 14th June 1913 there is a piece by Mr W H Hunt who mentions a mumming play as recalled by an inmate of the Stow-on-the-Wold workhouse who refers to this character as *Bells Abub*.

# 45. Souling Song – Tattenhall

Chorus: *A soul! A soul! A soulcake!*
*Please good missus, a soulcake!*
*An apple, a pear, a plum, or a cherry,*
*Any good thing to make us all merry,*
*One for Peter, two for Paul,*
*Three for Him who made us all.*

God bless the master of this house,
The mistress also,
And all the little children
That round your table grow.
Likewise young men and maidens,
Your cattle and your store;
And all that dwells within your gates,
We wish you ten times more.

Go down in the cellar
And see what you can find,
If the barrels are not empty
We hope you will prove kind.

We hope you will prove kind
With your apples and strong beer,
And we'll come no more a-souling
Till this time next year.

The lanes are very dirty
My shoes are very thin.
I've got a little pocket to put a penny in.
If you haven't got a penny
A ha'penny will do,
If you haven't got a ha'penny,
It's God bless you!

According to *English County Songs* (1893) by Lucy E Broadwood and J.A. Fuller Maitland, apart from the second half of verse two, which was restored from a Shropshire version*, 'the rest of the song was sung, exactly as it stands, by a little girl in Tattenhall School, in October, 1891.'*

# 46. The Spanish Lady's Love

Will you hear a Spanish Lady, how she wooed an Englishman?
Garments gay and rich as may be, decked with jewels she had on.
Of a comely countenance and grace was she,
And by birth and parentage of high degree.

As his prisoner there he kept her, in his hands her life did lie –
Cupid's bands did tie them faster by the liking of an eye.
In his courteous company was all her joy;
To favour him in anything she was not coy.

But at last there came the orders for to set the ladies free,
With their jewels still adorned, and free from harm or injury.
Then said the lady mild, 'Full of woe is me;
Oh, let me still sustain this kind captivity!'

'Gallant captain, show some pity to a lady in distress;
Leave me not within the city for to die in heaviness.
Thou hast this day set my body free,
But my heart a prisoner remains with thee.'

'How should you fair lady, love me, one who is your country's foe?
These fair words make me suspect you: serpents lie where flowers grow.'
'All the harm I wish to thee, most courteous knight,
God grant the same upon my head may light.'

'Blessed be the time and season that you came to Spanish ground;
If our foes you must be termed, then gentler foes we never found.
With our city you have won our hearts each one;
To your country bear away what is your own.'

'Rest you still, most gallant lady, rest you still, and weep no more;
Of fair lovers there are plenty – Spain does yield a wondrous store.
Though passion and jealousy may sieze their mind,
While an Englishmen is always counted kind.'

'Leave me not unto a Spaniard; you alone enjoy my heart.
I am lovely, young, and tender; and from you I would not part.
To serve thee day and night my heart is pressed:
For the wife of an Englishman is counted blessed.'

'I fear that it would be too cruel for to take a woman hence,
And an English soldier with a lady would be sure to cause offence.'
'I'll quickly change, myself, if this be so,
And like a page I'll follow thee where'er you go.'

'I have neither gold nor silver to maintain you in this case;
And travel carries many charges, as you know, in every place.'
'My chains and jewels all shall be thine own,
And five hundred pounds in gold that lies unknown.'

'On the seas are many dangers, many storms do there arise;
Which I fear you would find frightful, forcing tears from your bright eyes.'
'In truth I shall endure extremity,
For I'd gladly lose my life for thee.'

'Courteous lady, leave this fancy, here comes all that breeds the strife, -
In fair England I already have a woman to my wife.
I will not falsify my vow for gold or gain,
Nor yet the fairest flower in all of Spain.'

'Oh, how happy is the woman who enjoys so true a friend!
Many happy hours God send her – of my suit I'll make an end.
On my knees I crave a pardon for my sin,
Which from love and true affection did begin.

'Commend me to thy lovely lady, give to her this chain of gold,
And these bracelets as a token, grieving that I was so bold.
All of these fine jewels please take with thee,
They are fitting for your wife, but not for me.

'I will spend my days in prayer, love and all her wiles defy;
In a nunnery I will shroud me, far from any company.
But e'er my prayers do end, be sure of this,
To pray for thee and for thy love I will not miss.

So farewell, most gallant captain! Farewell too my hearts content!
Count not Spanish ladies wanton, though to thee my love was bent.
Joy and true prosperity go ever with thee!'
'The like fall ever to thy share most fair lady!'

The story goes that Sir Uryan Legh, of Adlington, fought at the siege of Cadiz in 1596 when a number of Spaniards were captured and a beautiful lady became his prisoner. On being released she declared her love for the chivalrous knight, and announced her intention of following him to England. It was only when he explained that he already had a wife waiting for him in Adlington that she unwillingly gave up the idea and decided to enter a convent instead.

The song was first registered as a broadside in 1603 (written by Thomas Deloney) and Dr J C Bridge mentions The Spanish Lady as being *'dramatised as a musical entertainment'* and presented at Covent Garden Theatre in 1765.

# 47. The Streams of Lovely Nancy

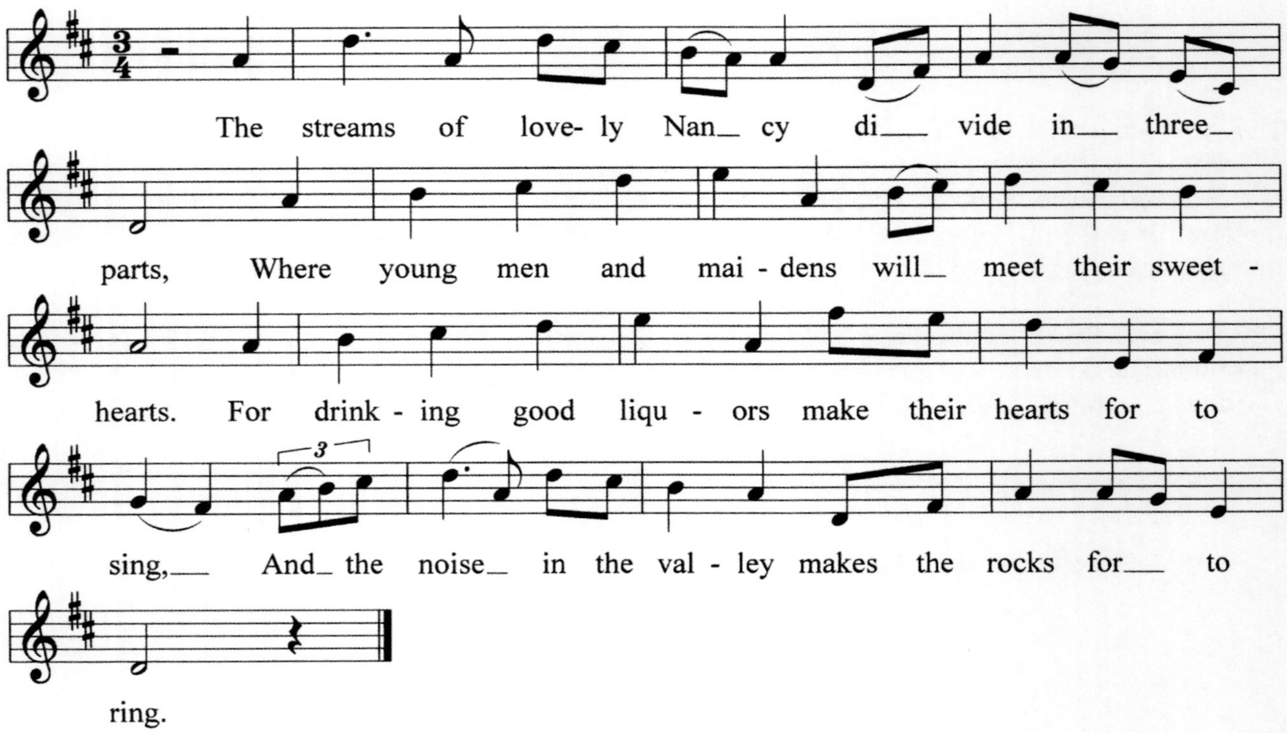


The streams of lovely Nancy divide in three parts,
Where young men and maidens will meet their sweethearts.
For drinking good liquors makes their hearts for to sing,
And the noise in the valley makes the rocks for to ring.

On yonder high mountains a castle does stand;
'Tis builded of ivory near to yon black strand.
'Tis builded of ivory and diamonds so bright,
It's a pilot for the sailors on a dark winter's night.

On yonder high mountain where wild fowls they fly,
There is one among them that flies very high;
If I had her in my arms near the diamond's black strand,
How soon I would secure her with the slight of my hand.

We marched from Chester to Liverpool town
And there we spied lasses, some fair and some brown,
But of all the fine lasses ever I did see
The voice of an angel is the darling for me.

Cecil Sharp collected this beautiful version from William Stokes at Chew Stoke, Somerset, in 1906, and I include it, if excuse were needed, purely because of the mention of Chester in the last verse. It was initially brought to my attention by Mary Humphreys after I heard her sing it at a festival in Eyam, Derbyshire. I think Mary sang some of the words slightly differently – a folk song will always adapt and change as it is sung – but I have returned to the text that Sharp collected with one exception. In verse 3 Mr Stokes sang *'If I had her on my gilgun or a night on the strand'* where I have used the more widely sung *'If I had her in my arms near the diamond's black strand'*.

## 48. The Tantivy Trot

Here's to the heroes of four-in-hand fame,
Harrison, Peyton, and Warde, sir;
Here's to the dragsmen that after them came,
Ford, and the Lancashire lord, sir.

Chorus: *Let the steam-pot hiss till it's hot;*
*Give me the speed of the Tantivy trot.*

Here's to the team, sir, all harnessed to start,
Brilliant in Brummagem leather;
Here's to the waggoner skilled in the art
Of coupling the cattle together.

Here's to the arm that holds them when gone,
Still to a gallop inclined sir;
Heads to the front with no bearing reins on,
Tails with no cruppers behind, sir.

Here's to the shape that is shown the near side,
Here's to the blood on the off, sir;
Limbs without check to the freedom of stride,
Wind without whistle or cough, sir.

Here's to the dear little damsels within,
Here's to the swells on the top, sir;
Here's to the music of three feet of tin,
Here's to the tapering top, sir,

Here's to the dragsmen I've dragged into song,
Salisbury, Mountain and Co., sir;
Here's to the Cracknell that cracks 'em along,
Five twenty times at a go, sir.

Here's to MacAdams, the Mac of all Macs,
Here's to the road we ne'er tire on;
Let me but roll o'er the granite he cracks,
Ride ye who like it on iron.

The Tantivy was the name of a coach service between London and Birmingham and this song, to the tune of *Here's To The Maiden of Bashful Fifteen*, was written in 1834 by R E Egerton Warburton of Arley. It was fashionable at the time for young men to be proficient in four in hand driving (the stagecoach was pulled by four horses so the drivers had four sets of reins to manage) and amateurs would often take the reins for part of a trip. For the professional drivers, who would be tipped by the amateur to hand him the reins, this was an extra source of income but often proved an inconvenience for the passengers, as the amateurs would drive the horses as fast as they dared giving a most uncomfortable ride. *Coupling the cattle* means harnessing the team, a *crupper* is a strap under the horse's tail and *three feet of tin* is a coach horn. *MacAdams* is a reference to John McAdam (1756 – 1836) who invented the macadam road surface and *on iron* is on the railway.

Egerton Leigh notes the following description of a stage coach journey and supposes it to be dated around 1765:

**The Stage Coach**

Resolved to visit a far distant friend,
A porter to the Bull and Gate I send,
And bid the slave at all events engage
Some place or other in the Chester stage.
The slave returns, 'tis done as soon as said,
Your honour's sure when once the money's paid.
My brother's whip, impatient of delay,
Puts to at three and swears he cannot stay,
(Four dismal hours ere the break of day)
Roused from sound sleep (thrice called) at length I rise,
Yawning stretching out my arms, half closed my eyes,
By steps and lanthorn enter the machine
And take my place – how cordially! – between
Two aged matrons of excessive bulk;
To mend the matter too, of meaner folk:
While in like mode jammed in on t'other side
A bullying captain and a fair one ride,
Foolish as fair, and in her lap a boy,
Our plague eternal, but her only joy.
At last, the glorious number to complete,
Steps in my landlord for that bodkin seat.
When soon by ev'ry hillock, rutt, and stone,
Into each other's face by turns were thrown;
This granam scolds; that, coughs; the captain swears;
The fair one screams, and has a thousand fears,
While our plump landlord, trained in other lore,
Slumbers at ease, nor yet ashamed to snore;
And master Dicky in his mother's lap,

Squalling at once brings up three meals of pap.
Sweet company! Next time I do protest, sir,
I'll walk to Dublin ere I ride to Chester.

He also mentions that in a similar ballad instead of taking his place *between two aged matrons of excessive bulk* the poor traveller is *squeezed in 'twixt two bolsters of talkative fat*.

# 49. There was an Old Farmer

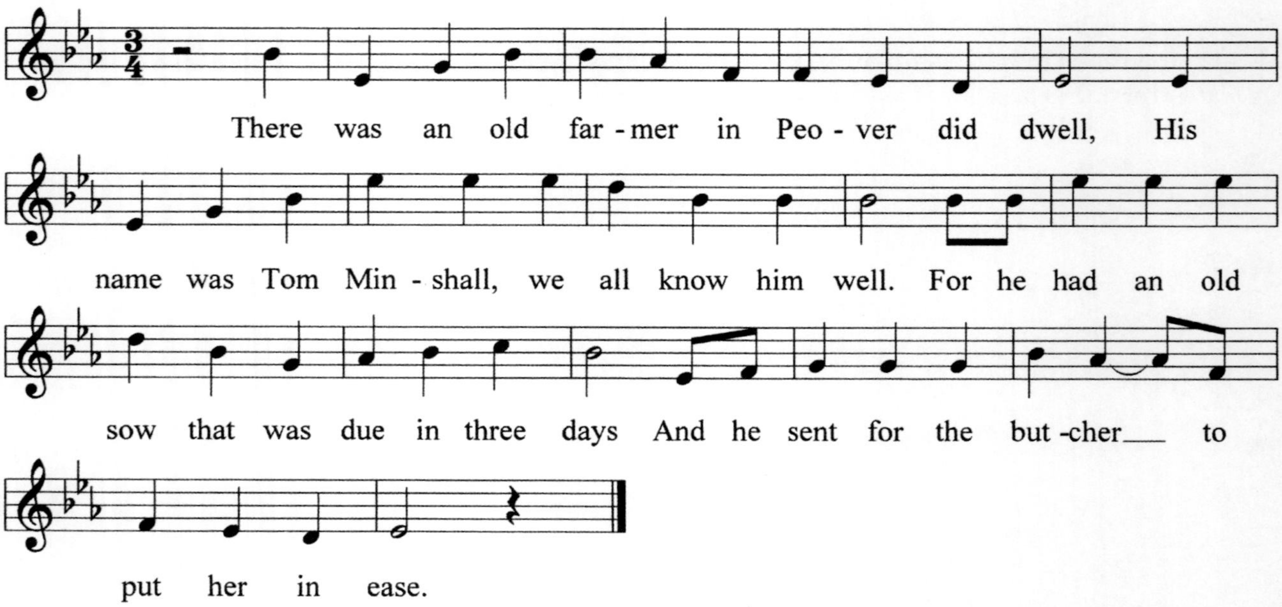


There was an old farmer in Peover did dwell,
His name was Tom Minshall, we all know him well.
For he had an old sow that was due in three days
And he sent for the butcher to put her in ease.

Oh, he sent for the butcher to put her in salt
And up comes the butcher, she ain't worth a groat.
Come butcher, come butcher, come do not deny,
She'll do to cut up and to make the lads pies.

Then in comes the Waggoner in a heck of a rage,
Come Master, come Master, come pay me my wage.
'Tis good luck to your horses, your harrows and plough,
For I ne'er will come back till you've e'tten owd sow.

Then in comes the Cowman in a heck of a stew,
Come Master, come Master, come pay me my wage.
'Tis good luck to your muck barrow, your shovel and brush,
For I ne'er will come back till you've e'tten 'Owd Sus'.

Then in comes the Milk Lad in a heck of a rage,
Come Master, come Master, come pay me my wage.
'Tis good luck to your milk horses, your float and your gig,
For I ne'er will come back till you've e'tten owd pig.

Then in comes the Servant in a heck of a rage,
Come Misses, come Misses, come pay me my wage.
'Tis good luck to your milk can, your shovel and brush,
For I ne'er will come back till thou's e'tten 'Owd Sus'.

Collected from Ted Staley of Over Peover by Duncan Broomhead, this song of an unscrupulous farmer has appeared in many versions. While the farmer believes he is on to a good thing, his work-force is clearly unimpressed by his attempt to feed them on unsuitable meat and decide to leave until they are sure that the danger has passed. Robert Holland, in a paper on rustic folklore for the Cheshire Archaeological Society in 1883, notes that farm servants who were not satisfied with the standard of their food would say:

*Brown bread and Mahley pies,*
*Twiggen Dick full o' eyes,*
*Buttermilk instead o' beer;*
*So I'll be hanged if I stay here.*

The fact that this is referred to as *'the Middlewich version'* implies that there were others and the mental picture of disgruntled farm workers flooding the countryside becomes difficult to avoid. *E'tten* means eaten, *mahley* is mouldy, *Twiggen Dick* is very hard skimmed milk cheese and the *eyes* are small pockets of rancid whey that appear in a badly made cheese.

The tune is a variant of the popular Victorian song *Villikins And His Dinah* (a cockney style version of an earlier broadside *William and Dinah*) and one that has been used for countless other songs and parodies. Some versions of *There Was An Old Farmer* use a *too-ra-li-oora-li-oora-li-ay* chorus, repeating the melody of the last line of the verse, but I haven't included it here as Ted didn't sing it.

## 50. Three Jovial Huntsmen

'Twas three jovial huntsmen and a-hunting they did go,
And they hunted and they halloed and they blew their horns also.
Look ye there.
They hunted and they halloed and the first thing they did find
Was a two-three children leaving school, and there they left behind.
Look ye there.
One said they were children, but another he said 'Nay,
They're nobbut little angels, let us leave them to their play.'
Look ye there.
They hunted and they halloed and the next thing they did find
Was an old sow lying in a ditch, and this they left behind.
Look ye there.
One said it were an old sow, but another he said 'Nay,
It's nobbut a Lunnon [London] Alderman that's gone and lost his way.'
Look ye there.
They hunted and they halloed and the next thing they did find
Was a gruntin', grindin' grindlestone, and this they left behind.
Look ye there.
One said it were a grindlestone, But another he said 'Nay,
It's nobbut an owd mowdy cheese as someone's thrown away.'
Look ye there.
They hunted and they halloed till the setting of the sun
And they'd nought to carry home again when the hunting day was done
Look ye there.
And one unto the other says 'This hunting doesn't pay,
But we'en powlet up and down a bit and had a rattlin' day.'
Look ye there.

From the library manuscript collection at Cecil Sharp House sent by D B Pemberton, of High Wycombe, Bucks, June 1960. The accompanying letter refers to it as *'The Three Jovial Huntsmen (Cheshire Version)'* and goes on to say *'I have called it a 'song', but I must admit that I never heard it sung.'*

Versions of this were widespread throughout Britain and America and concern a number of people, usually three, who bumble around the countryside to no great effect under the pretence of hunting. The first usually knows what they have found, the second contradicts him and the third thinks it is something completely different and often wholly improbable. The Roxburghe Ballads[6] collection contains a song beginning:

*There were three men of Gotam, as I have heard men say,*
*That needs would ride a hunting upon Saint David's day.*

Entitled *Choice of Inventions* and printed in 1632 it is probably one of the earliest versions.

[6] This is a collection of ballads, originally formed by Robert Harley, Earl of Oxford, and augmented by successive owners, among them John, Duke of Roxburghe, after whom the collection is now named. It is housed in the British Museum.

# 51. The Trees They Do Grow High

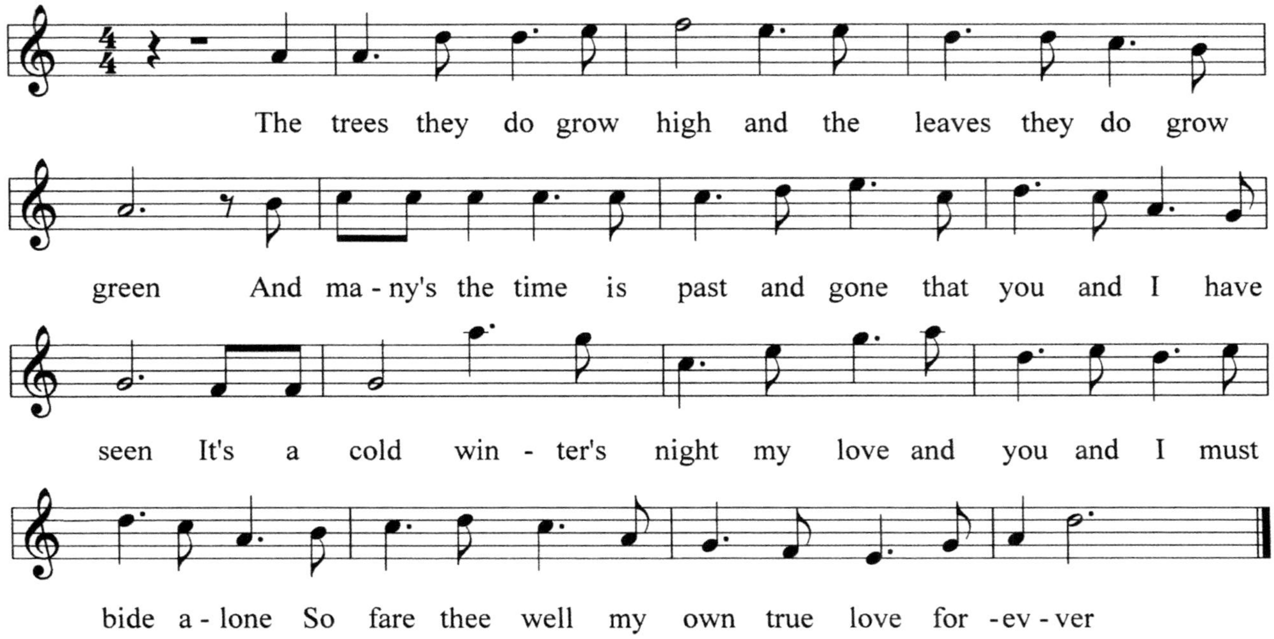


The trees they do grow high and the leaves they do grow green
And many's the time is past and gone that you and I have seen
It's a cold winter's night my love and you and I must bide alone
So fare thee well my own true love forever.

Oh father! Dearest father! I fear you've done me wrong
You've married me to a bonny boy but I fear he is too young
Oh daughter! Dearest daughter! If you will stay at home with me
A lady you will be while he's growing.

We'll send your love to college for one year or two
And then perhaps in time my love a man he may grow
We will tie a blue ribbon all around his bonny waist
To let the ladies know that he's married.

But at the age of fifteen he was a married man
And at the age of sixteen years the father of a son
But at the age of seventeen his grave it was a-growing green
Cruel death had put an end to his growing.

She sewed her love a shroud of the Holland Oh so fine
And every stitch she did put in the tears came trickling down
Oh once I had my own true love but now I've got never a one
So fare thee well my own true love forever.

The trees they do grow high and the leaves they do grow green
And many the time is past and gone that you and I have seen
It's a cold winter's night my love and you and I must bide alone
So fare thee well my own true love forever.

This was sung to me by Colin Haworth of the Eddisbury Fruit Farm in Kelsall. He learned it from his mother, Eleanor Mary Haworth, who sang it to him as a lullaby when he was a child. The theme is not uncommon throughout traditional song, but I find this a particularly haunting version.

## 52. The Two Brothers

'And it's where hast thou been all this night long, my son?
Come tell it unto me.'
'I have been lying on yonder bull-rushes,
Which lies beneath yond tree.'

'And it's what are the spots on this thy coat, my son?
Come tell it unto me.'
'They are the spots of my poor brother's blood,
Which lies beneath yonder tree.'

'And it's what didst thou kill thy poor brother for, my son?
Come tell it unto me.'
'Because he killed two pretty little birds,
Which flew from tree to tree.'

'It's what will thy father say when he comes, my son?
Come tell it unto me.'
'I will dress me up in sailor's clothes,
And my face he will never see.'

'And it's what will thou do with thy pretty little wife, my son?
Come tell it unto me.'
'I will dress her up in lad[d]ie's clothes,
And she will sail along with me.'

'And it's what wilt thou do with thy children three, my son?
Come tell it unto me.'
'I will leave them to my poor grandfather to rear,
And comfort [to] him [to be].'

'And it's when shall we see thy face again, my son?
Come tell it unto me.'
'When the sun and moon shines both at once,
And that shall never be.'

From *English and Scottish Popular Ballads* edited by Francis James Child (1825 - 96) and still regarded by many as the foremost work in this field. Child was born in Boston, graduated at Harvard University in 1846 and later became the university's first professor of English. He put together one of the largest folklore collections in existence and eventually published his book of ballads in five volumes between 1882 and 1898 (he completed the task except for a general introduction and bibliography). Of this song he says:

*'Communicated by Mr J K Hudson of Manchester. Sung after a St George play regularly acted on All Souls' Day at a village a few miles from Chester, and written down for Mr Hudson by one of the performers, a lad of sixteen. The play was introduced by a song called Souling and followed by two songs, of which this is the last, the whole dramatic company singing.'*

According to Anne Geddes Gilchrist in the *Journal of the English Folk Dance and Song Society* the village was Tarvin and the song was written down for Mr Hudson around 1891. She also notes that *'the Tarvin version* [of the souling play] *is remarkable for its introduction of two songs which have no connection with the play.'* These were *Jim The Carter Lad*, and the above song, which she refers to as

*Edward*, and is of particular interest, as she believed it to be the only traditional version recovered in England. This was probably so at the time but a few others have been collected since including one from Frank Hinchliffe, a fine traditional singer from south Yorkshire.

The bracketed suggestions in the text are Child's.

# 53. Um-Sta Doodle-Ay

I once was courting a nice young wench
And I courted her right well;
Her name was Molly-Rye-titty-fol-lol
And mine was Tommy Bell.
And every time I courted her,
Her father was always a-whoam
By Jing he swore if he catched me there
By Jingo he'd tickle my bum.

Chorus: *Oh, ee-dee, ay-dee, eye-dee, oh-dee, um-sta-dood-le-ay*
*Ee-dee, ay-dee, eye-dee, oh-dee, um-sta-dood-le-ay*

Now me and Molly Rye-titty-fol-lol
Arranged a little plan,
A ladder for to bring
To place again the window just proved the very thing.
We didn't joke, we didn't laugh,
But as the fun began
My foot slipped through the window
And I fell and cut my bum.

Now they wheeled me home in a wheelbarrow,
They wheeled me home with care.
My father and mother they were a-whoam
And ee how they did stare.

'What's the matter with our Tom,
What's the matter with our Tom?'
'Why the foo', he's been a courtin'
And he's fell and cut his bum.'

Now they whipped me off to the doctor,
The doctor studied my case.
I couldn't keep from laughing
When he stared me in the face.
'What a fool th'as made o' me.'
But a bigger foo' by gum
You should see the fool he made of me
When he turpentined my bum.

He took me into the surgery
I really spoke my mind,
When he got a mustard plaster
And he slapped it on behind.
And now when I'm walking down the street
Kids after me they run
Shouting 'There goes a man with his leg in a sling
And he's only got half a bum'.

A cautionary tale from the singing of Bob Rogers of Frodsham collected by Peter Kennedy. There are a number of songs from around the country on a similar theme including *Wop she 'Ad It-io* from the Copper family of Rottingdean in Sussex (world renowned for their traditional singing) and I have raided yet another version for the last verse. I always felt another verse would round the song off nicely and this one comes from the singing of the redoubtable Jim Eldon who earns his living entertaining the passengers on *The Yorkshire Belle*, a pleasure cruiser sailing out of Bridlington.

It is widely accepted with nearly all forms of folk music that the written form is really just a guide which allows scope for personal interpretation. This was never more the case than with this song as I had particular difficulty in taking down the tune from Bob's singing – largely because every verse was different. I feel, however, that I have successfully captured the essence of the melody that runs through his many variations.

# 54. The Unfortunate Loves of Thomas Clutterbuck and Polly Higginbotham

In Chester town a man there dwelt,
Not rich as Croesus, but a buck;
The pangs of love he dearly felt,
His name was Thomas Clutterbuck.
The lady he did most approve
Much guineas gold had got 'em,
And Clutterbuck fell deep in love
With pretty Polly Higginbotham.

Chorus: *Oh, Thomas Clutterbuck! Oh, Polly Higginbotham!*
*I sing the love, the smiling love Of Clutterbuck and Polly Higginbotham.*

A little trip he did propose,
Upon the Dee they got 'em;
The wind blew high he blew his nose
And sang to Polly Higginbotham.
The strain was sweet, the stream was deep,
He thought his notes had caught her;

But she alas! first fell asleep,
And then fell in the water.

Yet still he strained his little throat,
To love he did invite her,
And never missed until the boat
He thought went rather lighter;
But when he saw that she was gone,
The summum of his wishes,
He boldly paid the waterman
And jumped among the fishes.

Round Chester stalk the river ghosts
Of this young man and fair maid;
His head looks like a salmon-trout,
Her tail is like a mermaid.
Learn this, ye constant lovers all
Who live on England's island,
The way to shun a watery death
Is making love on dry land.

Described in Egerton Leigh's *Ballads and Legends of Cheshire* as simply *'a broadside'* (see *The Chester Garland*), though it is possible that this owes more to the influence of the music halls than anything else. Broadside ballads covered a wide range of subjects including complaints about poor working conditions and general political unrest, newsworthy events of the day, tales of love and intrigue and the countless Sorrowful Lamentations and Confessions of hanged men (as in *John Lomas's Farewell*). Not all of them, however, were tales of doom and gloom as this example illustrates admirably. It was a common ploy of broadside writers to set the words to a popular tune of the day, which made them easier to sell as the buyer did not have to be familiar with musical notation, and so, upholding the tradition, I have used the well-known air of *The British Grenadiers* here.

# 55. Welcome Cold November

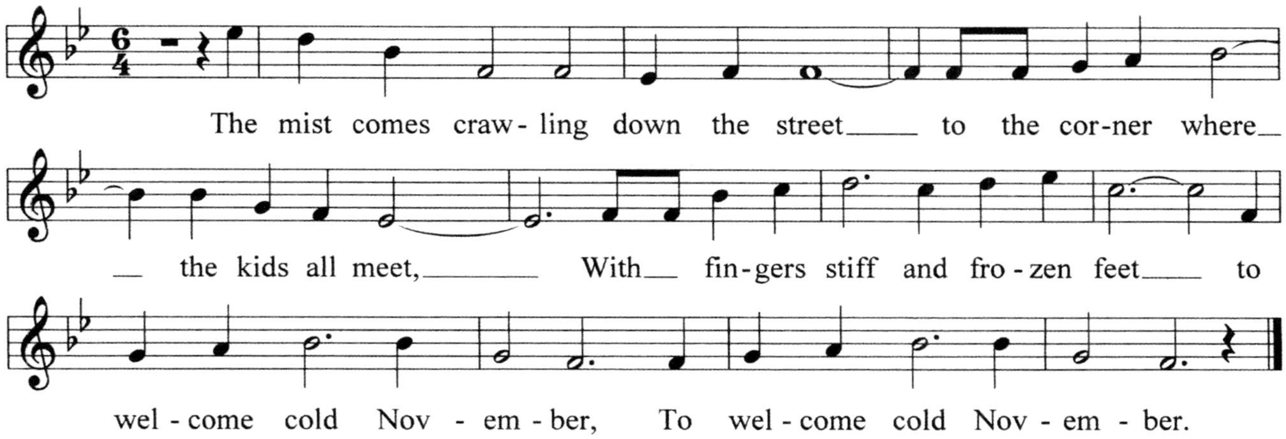


The mist comes crawling down the street
To the corner where the kids all meet,
With fingers stiff and frozen feet
To welcome cold November,
To welcome cold November.

And underneath the pale gaslight
We sang our songs into the night,
All down each alley sharp and bright,
To echo through November,
To echo through November.

Come rain or fog, you could be sure,
If you be rich or be you poor,
There'd come a knock upon your door,
It's only cold November,
It's only cold November.

And you never ask the reason why
You spared a penny for the guy,
Or roman candles in the sky,
To light up cold November,
To light up cold November.

And poor Guy Fawkes must burn again,
It's a pity that he died in vain,
For I should like to do the same,
To celebrate November,
To celebrate November.

But your father's standing at the gate,
And your mother's in a right old state,
Son, don't you know it's far to late
To wander through November,
To wander through November.

But now I'm old and past me prime,
Out of season out of rhyme,
The kids today can't find the time,
To welcome cold November,
To welcome cold November.

For an atmospheric description of a specific time of year and its attendant activities this song by Pete and Chris Coe is difficult to beat. Pete, who wrote the words, describes it as *'my childhood recollections of the '50s on Castle, Northwich'*. He goes on *'the song we sang was "This Night We Come a Soulcaking" prior to bonfire night then we'd hit the neighbours again, a week later, with "Penny for the Guy" – all very lucrative. The streets and alleys we roamed were gas lit and usually foggy (before the Clean Air Act) around Flower Street, Huxley Street and Romanes Street.* Currently residing in The Ryburn Valley in Yorkshire, he goes on to say *'Whilst I gather that Northwich is now quite upmarket it certainly wasn't in the '50s and '60s. There was still a lot of subsidence* [see *Salt Tell*, another of Pete's songs] *and we all lived in the shadow of ICI where my father worked. Very few of my friends stayed in the area beyond '64 – we couldn't wait to get out – and few of us ever return.'*

## 56. When I Was A Lad

When I was a lad as big as my Dad
I jumped into a tater bag.
The tater bag it was so full,
I jumped onto a roaring bull!
The roaring bull began to roar
And I jumped onto an old barn door.
The barn door began to crack
And I jumped onto a horse's back.
The horse's back began to bend,
And I jumped onto a turkey hen.
The turkey hen began to lay
And I jumped onto a load of hay.
The load of hay it was so nasty
I jumped onto an apple pasty.
The apple pasty was so good,
I ate it up as fast as I could!

I got this intriguing piece of nonsense rhyme from George Warrington of Mollington, who learned it from his mother during his childhood in Childer Thornton. It does not really have a tune as such but is recited in a rhythmical fashion.

# 57. Whistlebitch Well

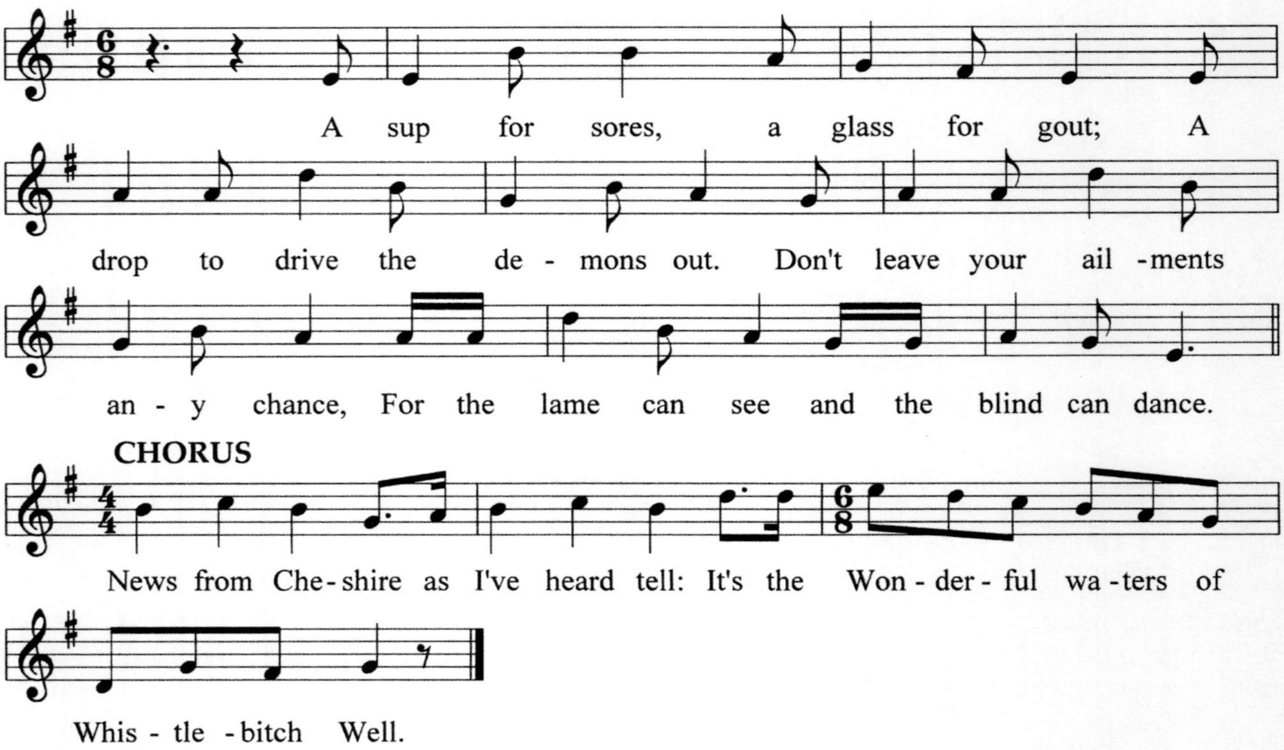


A sup for sores, a glass for gout;
A drop to drive the demons out.
Don't leave your ailments any chance,
For the lame can see and the blind can dance.

Chorus: *News from Cheshire as I've heard tell: It's the*
*Wonderful waters of Whistlebitch Well.*

The blacksmith caught a spark in his eye.
He loosed the mare which kicked his thigh.
He went to the well both blind and lame,
But he came dancing back again.

Now the chimney-sweep was rather shy,
Till he rubbed a drop upon each thigh.
What happened next we can't be sure
But he sweeps more chimneys than before.

When the parson got a boil on his bum
He couldn't sit, he couldn't run,
So he filled the font with this miracle cure
Where he sat and prayed to make quite sure.

Now Dr. Brown the truth to tell,
Fills his flask at the Whistlebitch Well.
Ten guineas a sip he will charge you,
He cured St. George and Slasher too.

So throw out your potions and your pills,
Powders cannot cure your ills.
All other treatments you must scorn,
Jump in the well tomorrow morning.

Whistlebitch Well is close to Tirley in the depth of Delamere Forest although the reality is somewhat less impressive than the legend. According to T A Coward (*Picturesque Cheshire*, 1903) the healing powers of the well were reported to be wonderful and any disease could be cured by drinking the waters. It is said that as many as two thousand people a day resorted to the spot to cure all manner of ills and the foresters had their work cut out trying to prevent the deer from being disturbed. The head forester would not allow any of his men to take fees from the sick, believing that such a marvellous cure should be free to all, but posted his men to avoid damage to adjoining property. Mr Coward also states that *'There is in the British Museum a rare pamphlet which was issued in 1600 describing "Newes out of Cheshire of the New found well"'* which he believes to be a reference to Whistlebitch. Although George Ormerod (*History of Cheshire,* 1882) does not mention the well as such he does include a map of Delamere Forest dated 1813 on which the well is clearly marked. It did not stand alone, however, as according to Ormerod *'mineral springs have been noticed in the accounts of Utkinton, Beeston and Spurstow, and since those accounts have been printed, others have been discovered in the neighbourhood of the Peckforton Hills.'* He also mentions a reference to a spring in Buglawton containing sulphur, Epsom salts and calcareous earth. That's bound to do you good!
The song was written by Pete Coe.

# 58. William and Mary

As William and Mary walked by the seaside,
Their last farewell to take,
'Should you never return,' young William she said,
'My poor heart will surely break.'

'Be not thus dismayed,' young William he said,
As he pressed the dear maid to his side,
'Nor my absence don't mourn, for when I return,
I will make little Mary my bride.'

Three years passed away without any news, when at last,
As she sat at her own cottage door,
An old beggar came by with a patch on his eye,
Quite lame, and did pity implore;

'If your charity you'll bestow,' said he,
'I will tell you your fortune beside,
The lad that you mourn will never return
To make little Mary his bride.'

Mary started and trembled,' O tell me,' she cried,
'All the money I've got I will give,
To what I ask you, if you will tell me true,
Only say, does my dear William live?'

'In poverty he lives,' said he,
'And shipwrecked he has been beside,
And return will no more, because he is poor,
To make little Mary his bride.'

'That he lives, Heaven knows the great joy that I feel,
Yet still his misfortunes I mourn,
For he'd been welcome to me in poverty,
In his blue jacket tattered and torn.

'For I love him so dear, so true and sincere,
That no other I swear beside,
If in riches he be rolled, and was clothed in gold,
Should make little Mary his bride.'

The patch from his eye the beggar then threw,
His old coat and his crutch too beside,
With cheeks like a rose, and in jacket so blue,
'Twas William stood by Mary's side.

'Forgive me, dear maid,' then William he said,
'Your love it was only I tried,
To church let's away, for ere the sun sets,
I'll make little Mary my bride.'

Many traditional songs follow the story of the parted lovers where the young man goes off to sea, to war, or on some other epic journey promising to marry his sweetheart on his return. They often contain the classic 'broken token' verses which requires a small object, usually a coin or a ring, to be cut in two with the lovers keeping half each so they will recognise each other after a lengthy absence. Others, like this one, rely on the girl not recognising her sweetheart at first but believing him (and resisting the urge to punch his lights out) when he reveals all after her love has been tested. This is from Barrett's *English Folk Songs*, the first verse and the tune come from Cheshire but the rest of the story has been filled out from a sheet ballad printed in 1794 by J Evans of Smithfield.

# 59. The Wizard of Alderley Edge

From Mobberley on a bright morning, on a snow-white pure-bred mare;
A farmer rode to Macclesfield for to sell her at the fair.
Over Alderley Edge he took his path where the day is endless night.
But the mare did halt in a shroud of mist, for a man all clad in white.

Chorus: *From Macclesfield to Mobberley if you have wares to sell,*
*Don't leave the path at the Wizard's Inn, or drink at the Wizard's Well.*

'Well met,' said the man as he stood in the path, 'Won't you sell to me your mare?'
But the farmer said, 'She's not for sale 'til I get to Macclesfield fair.'
'Well you can stand all day at the fair, but no bidding you will hear,
I'll await you in this very same place as the evening does draw near.'

Now this farmer was a puzzled man as he rode into Macclesfield town,
For admiring glances all that day could never fill his purse with crowns.
So he returned a bitter man as the sun fell in the sky,
And just as he had said that morn, this Wizard did draw nigh.

'Now you must sell to me your mare for silver and bright gold,'
And he led the farmer and his mare down a path both dark and cold.

And they passed through some Iron Gates and through a great rock wall,
Like moles they went, nigh double bent, 'til they came to the Sleeper's Hall.

With fear this farmer wide did gaze, and loudly he did moan,
For full-dressed knights each with one mount except for one alone.
'These are King Arthur's gallant men, who wait on England's need,
So fill your purse and leave your mare, and leave the Edge with speed.'

Though he left the Edge a very rich man, his story caused him pain,
And those who would search for the Iron Gates will search the Edge in vain.
But some do say that Old Nell Beck did find the Iron Gates,
But most say that she stricken was, with the March Hare as her mate.

According to legend a Mobberley farmer was taking his horse to Macclesfield market when an old man stepped out and offered to buy it. When the farmer refused he was told that he would not sell it that day. This proved true and that evening, still leading his horse, he met the old man on the Edge again. He was told to follow, which he did, until they came to a rock which the old man touched with a wand. Iron gates opened in the hillside and revealed a succession of caverns filled with sleeping men and white horses. He was informed that these were King Arthur and his warriors who would wake to save the country when the need arose. One horse was missing and his was needed to make up the numbers for which he was told to take what payment he wanted from the piles of gold lying in the cave. Neither the old man nor the door in the rock face was ever seen again. The old man was presumably Merlin the magician and, according to Frederick Woods in *Legends and Traditions of Cheshire* (1982), contemporary accounts put this incident as supposedly taking place around 1696.

The story was put into song by Pete Coe in 1972 and printed below is his revised version written in 2000.

There was a farmer lived in Mobberley, he had a snow-white pure-bred mare,
But times were lean and prices keen, he must sell her at the fair.
So he took the path over Alderley Edge in the early morning light
But waiting there in a cloud of mist, was a man all clad in white.

Chorus: *From Macclesfield to Mobberley if you have wares to sell,*
*Don't leave the path at the Wizard Inn, or drink at the Wizard's Well.*

His words came slow in a voice so low, 'Won't you sell to me your mare?'
But the farmer said, 'She's not for sale 'til I get to Macclesfield fair.'
'Well you may stand all day at the fair, but not one bid you'll hear,
For it is my fate, that I must wait, though it be for a thousand years.'

This farmer was a troubled man as he came into Macclesfield town,
For although the mare was much admired, no offers could be found.
So he returned a bitter man as the moon rose up the hill,
And just as he had said before, the Wizard was waiting still.

'Now you must sell your mare to me, for payment in pure gold,'
And he led the farmer and his mare down a path so dark and cold.
And they passed through some Iron Gates and through a great rock wall,
Like moles they went, nigh double bent, 'til they came to the Sleeper's Hall.

Now the sight that met the farmer's eyes, turned his heart to stone,
For full-dressed knights, each with a mount, except for one alone.
'This is King Arthur's Company, on England's call attend,
So fill your purse and leave your mare, on her we do depend.'

'Now leave this place, do not return and may your story bring you fame,
But those who seek the Iron Gates will search the Edge in vain."
But I was told that Old Nell Beck once found the Iron Gates,
But others say, her head's astray and the March Hare is her mate.

# 60. Young Bucks A-Hunting Go

How sweet is the horn that blows in the morn,
Young bucks a hunting go;
How sweet is the horn that blows in the morn,
Young bucks a hunting go,
Young bucks a hunting go;
All my fancy dwells upon Nancy While I sing tally ho!
While I sing tally ho!
All my fancy dwells upon Nancy while I sing tally ho!

The fox leaped over the hedges so high,
The hounds all after him go;
The fox leaped over the hedges so high,
The hounds all after him go,
The hounds all after him go;
All my fancy dwells upon Nancy,
While I sing tally ho, while I sing tally ho!
All my fancy dwells upon Nancy while I sing tally ho!

How sweet is my home, my low, little cot,
Let my station be high or low;
How sweet is my home, my low, little cot,
Let my station be high or low,
Let my station be high or low;

All my fancy dwells upon Nancy,
While I sing tally ho, while I sing tally ho!
All my fancy dwells upon Nancy while I sing tally ho!

Were she my wife, how sweet my life,
There's none but I can know;
Were she my wife, how sweet my life,
There's none but I can know,
There's none but I can know;
All my fancy dwells upon Nancy,
While I sing tally ho, while I sing tally ho!
All my fancy dwells upon Nancy while I sing tally ho!

This *'very musical hunting song'*, as Frank Kidson describes it, was sent to him by Mr Thomas Hewson of Roundhay. According to Mr Hewson it was commonly sung on the Cheshire, Staffordshire, and Shropshire borders between 1820 and 1840. The words and tune here are as sung by a follower of the Cheshire hounds of that period, except for the last verse which I added from a similar version printed in *A Garland of Country Songs*, by the Rev S Baring-Gould.

# INDEX OF FIRST LINES

# SOURCES OF THE SONGS

1. **Alderley Lasses, The:** From *Cheshire Notes and Queries* Vol 2, No 1, 1897, p14.

2. **Alderley Mummers Song:** From a performance of the Alderley Mummers Play. Recorded by Roy Clinging at the Waters Green Tavern, Macclesfield 8/1/99. The Vaughan Williams Memorial Library at Cecil Sharp House, London has a recording of Alec Barber (recorded by Mike Yates) singing this song and also reciting the full text of the play (VWMLCD 2).

3. **Blue Cap:** Words and music by Pete & Chris Coe. © Backshift Music.

4. **Brisk Young Widow, The:** The Vaughan Williams Memorial Library, Cecil Sharp House, London. Collected by Cecil Sharp from George Radford of Bridgwater Union, Somerset 22nd August 1905. Ms ref: folk words 664-666, folk tunes 582. Roud 2438.

5. **Cheshire Born:** Words and music by Roy Clinging 1997.

6. **Cheshire Cavalry:** From Egerton Leigh's *Ballads and Legends of Cheshire* (1867). Words adapted and tune written by Roy Clinging 1997.

7. **Cheshire Cheese:** Words and music from Egerton Leigh's *Ballads and Legends of Cheshire* (1867). Also *Cheshire Notes & Queries* Vol 2 No 2, 1897, p135.

8. **Cheshire Lads Are Chief of Men:** From *Cheshire Notes & Queries* Vol 1, Dec 1896, p173.

9. **Cheshire Man, The:** Recorded by Roy Clinging from Reg Holmes of Norley, 17/11/98.

10. **Cheshire Militia, The:** From the papers of Dr J C Bridge left to the Chester Archaeological Society. Reproduced with the permission of Cheshire Record Office ref: ZCR62/2/83.

11. **Cheshire Regiment:** Recorded by Roy Clinging from Jim Buckley of Moulton, Near Northwich, 9/5/2000.

12. **Chester Garland, The:** From the Firth Ballads (compiled by Charles Harding Firth), a collection of printed broadsides in the Special Collections and Library Archives of Sheffield University. By permission of the Librarian, University of Sheffield Library.

13. **Colin and Phoebe:** From *Traditional Tunes* (1891) by Frank Kidson.

14. **Congleton Bear, The:** Words and music by Pete Coe. © Backshift Music

15. **Curst Fisherman, The:** The text is from Egerton Leigh's *Ballads and Legends of Cheshire* (1867). The tune is by Roy Clinging.

16. **Devil and the Monk, The:** The text is from Egerton Leigh's *Ballads and Legends of Cheshire* (1867). Words adapted and tune written by Roy Clinging 1997.

17. **Farmer's Boy, The:** The first verse and tune recorded by Mike Yates from Ernest Collins of Altrincham, 1975. The rest of the text is from Mrs Holt, of Alderhill, as printed in *Traditional Tunes* (1891) by Frank Kidson.

18. **Froggie:** Words and music by the late Leslie Haworth of Kelsall. Learned from the singing of Colin Haworth, his son. © Essex Music

19. **Glorious Sixth of May, The:** From the papers of Dr J C Bridge left to the Chester Archaeological Society. Reproduced with the permission of Cheshire Record Office ref: ZCR62/2/81 & 83.

20. **I'm Afraid I Shall Never Be Married:** From the *Journal of the Folk Song Society* Vol 8, 1929, pp 142-143. Reproduced courtesy of the EFDSS.

21. **John Lomas's Farewell:** Broadside printed by G Coman of Nantwich, kindly sent to me by Roy Palmer.

22. **Joseph Baker:** Words by Pete Coe, the tune is a variant of *The Miller of the Dee.* © Backshift Music.

23. **Keys of Heaven, The:** Collected by the Rev S Baring-Gould from the Rev F Partridge and found in *Cheshire Notes and Queries,* Vol 4, No 1, 1899, pp 55-56. Also from *English County Songs,* (1893) by Lucy E Broadwood and J A Fuller Maitland.

24. **Lost Lady Found, The:** From *English Folk Songs* (1891) collected and arranged by William Alexander Barrett.

25. **Marlers' Song, The:** The text is from Egerton Leigh's *Ballads and Legends of Cheshire* (1867). Words adapted and tune written by Roy Clinging 1997.

26. **May Song - Cheshire:** Recorded by Roy Clinging from Reg Holmes of Norley, 17/11/98.

27. **May Song – Mobberley:** From *A Glossary of Some Words Used in the County of Chester,* by Robert Holland (c1830-93). Published for the English Dialect Society, 1886.

28. **Miller of the Dee, The:** Egerton Leigh's *Ballads and Legends of Cheshire* (1867) and *The Universal Songster* (n.d.) Vol 3, p 306.

29. **Navigator's New Victory, The:** From the Madden Collection, Cambridge University Library. Madden Collection 20 (Country Printers 5), item no. 1; Madden Collection (Slip Songs H-N), item no. 1197. Copies at Cecil Sharp House.

30. **Norley Gate, The:** Words by Reg Holmes, tune *The Wild Colonial Boy*.

31. **Old Man Outwitted, The:** From Egerton Leigh's *Ballads and Legends of Cheshire* (1867), but originally from *Palatine Anthology* by J O Halliwell (1850). The text, however, has been freely adapted and set to a tune written by Roy Clinging.

32. **Old Reynard's Got Away:** Words and music by Reg Holmes.

33. **Pace Egging Song:** Text noted by Venetia Newall in 1966 from Arthur Hulme (born 1886) of Marple, Cheshire; tune from a Cheshire source added by Roy Palmer (*English Country Songs,* 1986).

34. **Prentice Boy, The:** The manuscript collection of HED Hammond held at the Vaughan Williams Memorial Library, Cecil Sharp House, London. Reproduced courtesy of the EFDSS.

35. **Rambling Royal, The:** Collected by A L Lloyd from Frank Jeffries, a seaman, Liverpool 1938. In *Everyman's Book of British Ballads*, 1980, edited by Roy Palmer. Also in *What A Lovely War*, 1990, again edited by Roy Palmer.

36. **Remember:** The text is from *Cheshire Notes and Queries* Vol 3 No1, 1898, pp 59-60 in a section called *Poets Corner*, which appears to have been for local contributions. The tune is by Mal Waite.

37. **Rich Farmer in Cheshire, The:** Learned from Mal Waite and combined with material from other traditional sources. Other versions can be found in *The Constant Lovers* (1972) edited by Frank Purslow, *Everyman's Book of British Ballads* (1980) edited by Roy Palmer and Egerton Leigh's *Ballads and Legends of Cheshire* (1867).

38. **Rope Dance:** Words and music by Pete Massey and Gordon Morris 1995.

39. **Salt Tell:** Words and music by Pete & Chris Coe. © Backshift Music.

40. **Sands of Dee, The:** Words by Charles Kingsley (1819-75), tune by Roy Clinging.

41. **Shocklach Carol, The:** Collected by Brian Ballinger from Tom Clarke (words) and Mr J S Sudlow (music) of Shocklach, Cheshire, in December 1957. Sent to me by Duncan Broomhead.

42. **Souling Song:** *Journal of the English Folk Dance and Song Society,* Vol 3, 1938, p 203. Contributed by Miss Witham of Chester. Reproduced courtesy of the EFDSS.

43. **Souling Song – Guilden Sutton:** *Journal of the English Folk Dance and Song Society* Vol 5, 1947, pp 85-91. Contributed by Catherine

Cathcart-Smith. Reproduced courtesy of the EFDSS.

**44. Souling Song – Stapleford:** Collected by Duncan Broomhead from Mr James Henry (Harry) Lee of Kelsall June/August 1978.

**45. Souling Song - Tattenhall:** *English County Songs* (1893) by Lucy E Broadwood and J A Fuller Maitland.

**46. Spanish Lady's Love, The:** Egerton Leigh's *Ballads and Legends of Cheshire* (1867).

**47. Streams of Lovely Nancy, The:** The Vaughan Williams Memorial Library, Cecil Sharp House, London. Collected by Cecil Sharp from William Stokes at Chew Stoke, Somerset on 29th August 1906 (as *Lovely Nancy*). Ms ref: folk words 1092-1093, folk tunes 1092. Roud 688.

**48. Tantivy Trot, The:** Written by R E Egerton Warburton (1803-91) of Arley. Sent to me by Roy Palmer and also in *Strike The Bell* (Cambridge, 1978) edited by Roy Palmer.

**49. There was An Old Farmer:** Collected by Duncan Broomhead from Ted Staley of Over Peover, 1982. The second verse has been reinstated from a version collected from James Henry (Harry) Lee of Kelsall, also by Duncan Broomhead, in 1978.

**50. Three Jovial Huntsmen:** Sent by D B Pemberton to the English Folk Dance and Song Society and held in the manuscript collection at the Vaughan Williams Memorial Library, Cecil Sharp House, London. Reproduced courtesy of the EFDSS.

**51. Trees They Do Grow High, The:** Recorded by Roy Clinging from Colin Haworth of Kelsall 6th March 1999.

**52. Two Brothers, The:** From *English and Scottish Popular Ballads, Vol 5 Additions and Corrections* (1894-98) edited by Francis James Child, where it is called *The Twa Brothers*. Also in the *Journal of the English Folk Dance and Song Society* Vol 3, 1938, pp 205-206, as *Edward*.

**53. Um-Sta-Doodle-Ay:** Collected by Peter Kennedy from Bob Rodgers 1st November 1954. Reproduced by kind permission of *Folktracks and Soundpost Publications*. The last verse is from the singing of Jim Eldon.

**54. Unfortunate Loves of Thomas Clutterbuck and Polly Higginbotham, The:** Egerton Leigh's *Ballads and Legends of Cheshire* (1867). Words adapted by Roy Clinging, tune *The British Grenadiers*.

**55. Welcome Cold November:** Words by Pete Coe and music by Chris Coe. © Backshift Music

**56. When I Was A Lad:** Recorded by Roy Clinging from George Warrington of Mollington 17th January 2005.

**57. Whistlebitch Well:** Words and music by Pete Coe. © Backshift Music

**58. William and Mary:** From *English Folk Songs* (1891) collected and arranged by William Alexander Barrett.

**59. Wizard of Alderley Edge, The:** Words and music by Pete Coe 1972 © Backshift Music. New words Pete Coe 2000.

**60. Young Bucks A-Hunting Go:** From *Traditional Tunes* (1891), by Frank Kidson. I have added the last verse from a similar version printed in *A Garland of Country Songs* (1895) collected and arranged by the Rev S Baring-Gould and H Fleetwood Sheppard.

# BIBLIOGRAPHY

Axon, William E A. *Cheshire Gleanings.* Manchester: Tubbs, Brook & Chrystal, London: Simpkin, Marshall & Co, 1884.

Barber, Edward, and P H Ditchfield. *Memorials of Old Cheshire.* George Allen & Sons, London, 1910.

Baring-Gould, S, and H Fleetwood Sheppard. *A Garland of Country Songs.* London, Methuen & Co., 1895.

Barrett, William Alexander. *English Folk Songs.* London, Novello, Ewer & Co., [1891].

Bridge, Joseph C. *Cheshire Proverbs and Other Sayings and Rhymes.* Chester: Phillipson & Golder, London: Simpkin, Marshall, Hamilton, Kent & Co. Ltd., 1917.

Broadwood, Lucy E and J A Fuller Maitland. *English County Songs.* The Leadenhall Press, London, 1893.

Chappell, W, and Ebsworth, J W. *The Roxburghe Ballads.* A published selection in nine volumes. Hertford 1871-99.

*Cheshire Notes and Queries.* Volumes 1 - 6, 1896-1901.

Child, Francis James. *English and Scottish Popular Ballads.* 5 volumes, New York Dover publications, 1965, first published 1882-1898.

Coward, T A. *Picturesque Cheshire.* Sherratt & Hughes, London and Manchester, 1903.

Crossley, F H. *Cheshire.* Robert Hale Ltd., London, 1949.

Darlington, Thomas. *The Folk Speech of South Cheshire.* Published for the English Dialect Society, 1887.

Gamlin, Hilda. *Memories of Birkenhead.* Edward Howell, Liverpool, 1892.

Helm, Alex. *Cheshire Folk Drama.* The Guizer Press, Ibstock, Leicester, 1968.

Hole, Christina. *Traditions and Customs of Cheshire.* Williams & Norgate Ltd., London, 1937.

Holland, Robert. *A Glossary of Words Used in the County Of Chester.* Published for the English Dialect Society, London, Trubner & Co., 1886.

Kidson, Frank. *Traditional Tunes.* Charles Taphouse & Son, Oxford, 1891.

Leary, Frederick. *The Earl of Chester's Regiment of Yeomen Cavalry 1797 to 1897.* Private publication, Ballantyne Press, Edinburgh, 1898.

Leigh, Egerton. *Ballads and Legends of Cheshire.* Longmans & Co., London, 1867.

Leigh, Egerton. *Glossary of Words Used in the Dialect of Cheshire.* London: Hamilton, Adams & Co., Chester: Minshull & Hughes, 1877.

Lloyd, A L. *Folk Song in England.* Lawrence and Wishart, London, 1967.

Moss, Fletcher. *Folklore, Old Customs and Tales of My Neighbours.* Private publication, 1898.

Nield, Maureen. *Rope Dance.* Cheshire County Council (Libraries & Archives), Manchester, 1993.

Ormerod, George. *The History of the County Palatine and City of Chester.* George Routledge & Sons, London, second edition 1882.

Palmer, Roy. *English Country Songbook.* Omnibus Press, 1986, first published 1979.

Palmer, Roy. *Everyman's Book of British Ballads.* J. M. Dent & Sons, London, 1980.

Purslow, Frank. *The Constant Lovers.* EFDS publications Ltd., New Bond Street, London, 1972.

Samuel, Raphael. *Miners, Quarrymen and Saltworkers.* Routledge & Keegan Paul Ltd., London, 1977.

Sharp, Cecil J. *Folk Songs of Somerset.* Simpkin & Co., London, 1904.

*The Cheshire Round.* 1960-1969.

*The Cheshire Sheaf.* Volume 1 (first series) - Volume 4 (third series), May 1878 - Dec 1902

*The Universal Songster.* 3 volumes. George Routledge & Sons, London, n.d.

Wilbraham, Roger. *An Attempt at a Glossary of Some Words Used in Cheshire.* London, T Rodd, 'second edition with considerable additions' 1826.

Woods, Frederick. *Legends and Traditions of Cheshire.* Shiva Publishing Ltd., Nantwich, 1982.

Woods, Frederick. *Further Legends and Traditions of Cheshire.* Shiva Publishing Ltd., Nantwich, 1983.

# ACKNOWLEDGEMENTS

There are many people without whose help, co-operation, inspiration and encouragement this collection would not have been possible. A large number have sent me songs and information, for which I am extremely grateful, and they are duly mentioned in the relevant sections of the main text. There are others, however, whose help has been clearly above and beyond the call of duty. They are:

**Roy Palmer, Duncan Broomhead** and **Pete Coe** who have all contributed immensely with research and presentation of material.

**Malcolm Taylor** and the **Vaughan Williams Memorial Library.** Apart from being an invaluable resource the staff have given help and assistance beyond all expectations.

**Adrian Sumner**, Chester City Council Arts Officer, and **Nicky Duirs** and **Audrey Siddall** of Cheshire County Council for support and sponsorship.

**Sue Jones, Catriona Thompson** and **Cheryl Hunt** for assistance with workshops and transcribing musical notation and **Andrew Nixon** for his expert advice in transferring the music to the printed page and correcting all my errors.

**Roger Stephens** for his creative and specially drawn map.

**Anne & Jack Loader** for their knowledge and experience in setting the whole thing up and letting me know what is and isn't possible in a book of this type.

**Mike Raven** without whose initial encouragement I might never have done it at all.

There are also a goodly number of people who have kindly allowed me to reproduce copyrighted material for which I am extremely grateful. They are:

**Peter Kennedy, Pete Coe, Reg Holmes, Mike Yates, Brian Ballinger, Roy Palmer, Colin Haworth, Richard Haworth, Giles Haworth, Mal Waite, Peter Massey, Gordon Morris, The English Folk Dance & Song Society, Cheshire Record Office.**

While I have made every effort to contact all copyright holders, if anyone is aware of any omissions in this respect I would be grateful if they could inform me so that details can be rectified in future editions.